THE TROUBLE

WITH

SIOP®

The Trouble with
SIOP®

How a Behaviorist Framework,
Flawed Research, and
Clever Marketing
Have Come to Define
– and Diminish –
Sheltered Instruction for
English Language Learners

Featuring an Alternative Approach to Sheltered Instruction
and a Sample Unit Applying That Framework

By James Crawford &
Sharon Adelman Reyes

Institute for Language & Education Policy

PORTLAND, OREGON

For permission to reprint, send email to:
pubs@elladvocates.org
Or send postal mail to:
ILEP
P.O. Box 19025
PORTLAND, OR 97280

A trademarked name, SIOP,® appears throughout this book. Rather than include a trademark symbol with every occurrence, the book uses "SIOP" in an
editorial fashion, with no intention of infringement of the owner's trademark.

ISBN 978-0-9861747-0-4

Library of Congress Control Number: 2014919731
Library of Congress Subject Headings:

1. English language—Study and teaching (Elementary)—Foreign speakers
2. Second language acquisition—Study and teaching (Elementary).
3. Constructivism (Education)—United States.
4. Immersion method (Language teaching).
5. Education, bilingual—Study and teaching (Elementary).

Cover photograph by Lewis Hine
Courtesy of the Library of Congress, LC-DIG-nclc-04529

Book design and typography by James Crawford

Printed in the United States of America
First edition

10 9 8 7 6 5 4 3 2 1

Contents

Preface vii

Introduction 1

Chapter One
A Rationale for Sheltering 3
    Theoretical Framework 5
    Why Have Traditional Methods Failed? 7
    Back to Behaviorism 9

Chapter Two
What Is SIOP? 11
    Valid and Reliable? 13
    Best Practices or Worst? 14

Chapter Three
'Research-Based' Hype 16
    Fidelity Study 18
    Science Study 19
    Writing Study 21
    New Jersey Study 22
    Reading Study 24
    Bottom Line 25

Chapter Four

SIOP in Theory: Teaching by Numbers 27

   Philosophical Muddle 29

   Corrupting Krashen 31

   Dumbing It Down 35

   Who Needs Theory? 36

Chapter Five

SIOP in the Classroom: Micromanaging Instruction . . . 37

   Lesson Preparation 38

   Building Background 39

   Comprehensible Input 41

   Strategies 43

   Interaction 44

   Practice & Application 45

   Lesson Delivery 47

   Review & Assessment 48

   'TWIOP' 50

Chapter Six

Conclusions 55

Appendix A

The ENGAGE Framework 59

   What Is Constructivism? 62

   Sheltering 62

   Scaffolding 63

   Classroom Environment 65

Appendix B

Discovering the Amazon: A Middle School Unit 71

References 83

About the Authors 89

Preface

Today's teachers have many concerns: high-stakes testing, punitive accountability systems, top-down standards, narrowed curricula, unfair evaluation schemes, punitive "restructuring" and school closures, draconian budget cuts, limits on collective bargaining rights, attacks on tenure, staff layoffs, salary freezes ... the list of misguided policies goes on.

One policy in particular is generating concerns among the educators of English language learners. An approach known as the Sheltered Instruction Observation Protocol, or SIOP,® is being adopted in a growing number of school districts across the United States. Reviews have been mixed. Some teachers, especially those with limited experience in working with English learners, have welcomed the detailed guidance that SIOP provides. But SIOP's prescriptiveness has also brought complaints: that it stifles creativity in the classroom, fails to engage students, and serves as a tool for micromanaging student learning.

The SIOP® Model has been spreading for more than a decade, due in part to a political backlash against bilingual education. Seeking to avoid controversy, many school districts now prefer all-English approaches for teaching English learners. SIOP allows the use of students' native language "to clarify key concepts as needed,"[1] but even that minimal form of bilingualism is optional. Monolingual English instruction normally prevails. Until recently, we had viewed SIOP as merely one among many prepackaged "learning systems" that tout themselves as "research-based" and compliant with No Child Left Behind, Race to the Top, and the Common Core State Standards. Hardly a new phenomenon. One can only hope that schools will maintain a buyer-beware approach.

So why have we now decided to take a closer look at SIOP? For three reasons.

First, teachers are telling us that its rigid formula for instruction leaves them feeling frustrated and disempowered. Some say they are being forced to abandon methods that have worked well with English learners

[1]SIOP Feature 19; Echevarría et al. (2013), p. 157.

in the past. Others resent being evaluated on whether they incorporate SIOP's "30 features and eight components" into every lesson, every day. And many question whether such a high degree of conformity is necessary or desirable in teaching their students. How justified are these reactions?

Second, SIOP comprises a heterogeneous mix of methodologies, strategies, and techniques, most of which are not specific to teaching English learners. We wondered: Is this truly a model of sheltered instruction? Does it flow from a theoretical understanding of second language acquisition? Is it based on a consistent educational philosophy? Or is it merely a grab-bag of so-called "best practices"?

Finally, as best we can determine, the impact of SIOP on students has been less than impressive. How valid are the claims about its effectiveness? The federal Institute of Education Sciences (IES), which funded the development and much of the research on SIOP, says that no evaluation study of the model conducted thus far meets its "evidence standards." Thus the What Works Clearinghouse at IES "is unable to draw any conclusions based on research about the effectiveness or ineffectiveness of SIOP on English language learners."[2] Yet this determination seems to have done nothing to diminish SIOP's influence—or the high-powered advertising behind it.

One might reasonably ask: How can SIOP's sponsors justify advertisements claiming that their product is "scientifically validated"? True, it has been the subject of a few research studies (mainly by the SIOP authors themselves, who have a professional and financial stake in the results). But what does this research actually show? Does the model live up to the claims of its proponents? Or is it a step in the wrong direction?

Since a growing number of English learners are directly affected by SIOP, we believe these questions deserve more attention than they have thus far received. Hence this book.

The opinions, judgments, and conclusions expressed here are entirely our own. At the same time, we gratefully acknowledge the assistance of Stephen Krashen, professor emeritus at the University of Southern California. As the linguist who proposed the first comprehensive theory of

[2]Institute of Education Sciences (2013), p. 1.

second language acquisition, developed the concept of *comprehensible input,* and elaborated a methodology known as *sheltered subject matter instruction,* Dr. Krashen is uniquely situated to analyze the scientific evidence on SIOP. As you will see, his insights are fascinating as well as troubling. We also thank Dr. Mary Carol Combs, associate professor of practice at the University of Arizona College of Education and a specialist in sheltered instruction, for reviewing a draft of this book and offering helpful suggestions.

THE TROUBLE WITH SIOP®

Introduction

Market dominance begins with branding, and the most successful brands become synonymous with the products they represent. Think of Kleenex® for tissue, Coke® for cola, and Xerox® for photocopy, to name a few. Now that education is a multibillion-dollar business in the United States, the branding phenomenon for school products and services should come as no surprise. Among the latest of these is SIOP,® a pedagogical approach that's fast becoming the dominant model of "sheltered instruction" for English language learners in this country.

An acronym for Sheltered Instruction Observation Protocol, SIOP was developed by researchers at a nonprofit organization and a university under contract with the U.S. Department of Education. It continues to be closely identified with the Center for Applied Linguistics, the nonprofit group, which specializes in language-related research, testing, and teacher training. What is less widely known is that, in 2004, this taxpayer-funded pedagogy was privatized, trademarked, and acquired by Pearson, a British publishing conglomerate that describes itself as "the world's leading education company." Indeed, Pearson's income from education alone was $7.3 billion in 2012, more than the education revenues of McGraw-Hill, Houghton Mifflin Harcourt, Cengage Learning, Santillana, Scholastic, and Blackboard combined. Two-thirds of Pearson's school-related profits come from the North American market, in which SIOP training and publications represent a growing share.[3] SIOP is being promoted internationally as well, as an all-purpose model of language teaching.[4]

According to the company, SIOP is "the only scientifically validated model of sheltered instruction ... a proven pedagogical approach to teaching both content knowledge and language skills [that] has helped

[3] In addition to producing numerous standardized tests, including the PARCC assessment aligned to the Common Core State Standards, Pearson owns a long list of publishing companies including Scott Foresman, Penguin, Addison-Wesley Longman, Prentice Hall, and Allyn & Bacon.
[4] Pearson (2012).

instruct millions of students."[5] The Center for Applied Linguistics sends a similar message, hailing SIOP as "a research-based and validated model that has been widely used across the U.S. for over 15 years. ... In addition, teachers report that SIOP-based teaching benefits all students, not just those who are learning English as an additional language."[6]

For schools struggling to respond to the needs of English language learners—and to raise their scores in an era of high-stakes testing—such advertisements can be alluring. They imply that if educators carefully follow a step-by-step recipe, developed and perfected by experts, superior results are virtually guaranteed. "Achievement gaps" will start to disappear, as children with limited English skills perform well on English-language tests. In the lingo of the No Child Left Behind Act, schools will finally "make AYP"[7] and administrators will get their bonuses (or at least get to keep their jobs).

Yet extravagant claims like these often disappoint, especially when it comes to teaching and learning. We think they deserve close scrutiny.

---

[5]Pearson (n.d.a, 2010). Its web site also claims that SIOP is now being used by more than 450,000 educators in U.S. schools.

[6]Center for Applied Linguistics (n.d.a, n.d.b).

[7]Adequate yearly progress.

1

A Rationale for Sheltered Instruction

WHAT IS SHELTERED INSTRUCTION? To answer this question—and dispel some of the confusion surrounding the term—a bit of background is required.

First, bear in mind that it can be challenging to teach a second language to anyone. Even more so to teach academic subjects in that language while your students are still struggling to learn it and you are being "held accountable" for their progress through constant testing. Add to that the complications of poverty, discrimination, family separation, low levels of literacy, poor health care, inadequate nutrition, and casual violence that often plague minority communities, creating a high-stress environment for children, and you'll begin to appreciate what it can mean to educate English language learners.

At one time, many U.S. schools addressed these challenges with bilingual education, an approach that provided a gradual transition from native language to mainstream classrooms. While such programs varied in quality, they were a major improvement on all-English "submersion" models, in which more children sank than swam. The better bilingual programs could also keep students from falling far behind while they acquired English, improving their chances for success in school. Then came a political backlash in the form of "English Only" activism, which targeted bilingual schooling for elimination. In 1998, Californians passed Proposition 227, a ballot measure that severely limited the use of native language instruction in public schools. Arizona and Massachusetts voters soon followed suit. The new laws mandated, as a default program for English learners, "sheltered English immersion during a temporary transition period not normally intended to exceed one year."[8] Feeling the political heat, other states and school districts began to favor all-English approaches as well. Ironically, a growing number of native-English speakers now benefit from "two-way" bilingual education designed to cultivate proficiency in two languages. Yet these programs serve only a tiny minority of English learners.

Does this mean that sheltered instruction is essentially an alternative to bilingual instruction? Not necessarily. While it can take that form, as it does in most SIOP classrooms, the origin of the concept was quite different. In fact, sheltered instruction was part of an effective, late-exit model of bilingual education that was pioneered in California more than 30 years ago. Children started out learning school subjects in their vernacular, then gradually moved into all-English classrooms taught at a level they could understand. By 4th or 5th grade, when they had acquired full or near-full proficiency in English, students began to join mainstream classrooms.[9] Despite the promise of these programs, however, most were scaled back or eliminated by Proposition 227.

Of course, native language instruction is not always feasible for English learners. Nor is it essential to the success of sheltered instruction. In a variety of contexts, sheltered approaches have consistently proved more effective than language teaching methods that stress direct instruction in grammar and vocabulary.[10]

An early example of sheltering dates from the mid-1960s. Anglophone parents in a suburb of Montreal complained that their children were being subjected to 12 years of mandatory instruction in French, yet rarely learned to use the language for any meaningful purpose. They

[8]California Education Code, §305.
[9]Crawford (2004).
[10]Krashen (1991).

demanded, and ultimately won, an alternative approach known as *French immersion,* in which students learned French as they studied school subjects in the second language. The superiority of this program model, as compared to traditional foreign language instruction, soon became obvious. By the end of elementary school, researchers found, the English-background students achieved high levels of competence in French at no cost to their academic progress. These were among the most dramatic results ever achieved in the field of language teaching, and they were confirmed by numerous studies.[11] It's no wonder that French immersion programs have become popular throughout Canada.

The question was *why*—what made immersion so effective?—and the answer was not so obvious. Was it massive exposure to French that made the difference? Or was it that students, placed in a "sink or swim" situation, were forced to speak the language on a daily basis? Perhaps a happy combination of teaching methods—"best practices"—was partly responsible. Maybe an ideal student-teacher ratio? High expectations for achievement? Grouping of students by language and ethnicity? A culturally relevant curriculum? Strong parental involvement and support for bilingualism? There were many possibilities.

Theoretical Framework

TO ANSWER THE EFFECTIVENESS QUESTION, it was not sufficient merely to describe and catalog the features of French immersion programs. To isolate the key variables that made them work, a practical *theory of second language acquisition* was required. A lively debate among linguists ensued and several theories emerged. The most explanatory and influential of these has been the Comprehension Hypothesis,[12] elaborated by Stephen Krashen in the early 1980s. It holds that one factor above all is responsible for second language acquisition: *comprehensible input* in that language.

In other words, what made French immersion successful was not the quantity of French input, but its quality. While engaged in the study of math or history or science, students were exposed to the language in a form they could understand. This was done by using French in mean-

[11]Cummins (2001 [1979]).
[12]Originally known as the Input Hypothesis.

ingful contexts. The more children focused on messages with a real-life purpose, rather than on, say, repetitive grammar drills or artificial dialogues, the more French they understood. And the more French they understood, the more French they acquired: incidentally, unconsciously, and effortlessly. This was not unlike the way young children acquire their first language: naturally, without the aid of flash cards and worksheets and without constant correction by adults.

French immersion classrooms differed in significant ways from sink-or-swim environments, in which a new language is perceived mostly as incomprehensible noise. Immersion teachers adjusted their use of French to make it accessible to students. They did this through careful choice of vocabulary, syntax, pacing, and intonation, and by avoiding needless complexity, making points directly rather than elliptically, and adding redundancy. Other techniques included contextual cues such as gestures, facial expressions, and body language.

Krashen described these adaptations, when applied consistently, as *sheltered subject matter instruction.*[13] Soon they were being used in U.S. bilingual programs, as noted above, and also in nonbilingual programs for teaching English. The important thing, Krashen stressed, was that sheltered instruction should focus students' attention on academic content and not on language. Teachers needed to emphasize the message, not the medium. Ideally, the curriculum should be so engaging that students would forget which language the teacher was using! As long as input was comprehensible, they would learn subject matter consciously while acquiring language *sub*consciously.

Another factor in the success of French immersion, Krashen postulated, was the exclusion of native-French-speaking students. The linguistic composition of the classroom, restricted to second language learners, made teachers constantly aware of the need to shelter their French to make it understandable at or near the level of the class. This also created a relaxed learning environment, reducing students' stress levels. They all made errors in French and, without the presence of native speakers of French, errors were less cause for embarrassment. The result was to

---

[13]Variants included *sheltered classes* and *sheltered subject matter teaching;* Krashen (1984, 1985, 1991).

lower what Krashen has termed the *affective filter*, a psychological barrier that can keep comprehensible input from "getting through."[14]

It is unnecessary, he added, to pressure students to produce speech or writing in the second language before they are ready, because "output" contributes nothing. It is the result of second language acquisition, not the cause. In fact, putting pressure on children to speak or write can be counterproductive, increasing stress and raising the affective filter.

Sheltered approaches have proved effective with older learners as well. In just one of several studies, Krashen and his colleagues found that university students in sheltered psychology classes made significantly greater progress in a second language than their counterparts in traditional foreign language classes, while learning just as much psychology as students taught in their first language.[15] Such findings provide further support for the Comprehension Hypothesis.

Why Have Traditional Methods Failed?

PARADOXICALLY, *NOT* FOCUSING ON LANGUAGE turns out to be an effective way to teach language in sheltered classrooms, especially the kind of academic language that students need for school. By contrast, "skill-building" approaches, which feature explicit instruction in the formal aspects of language, have a poor record of success. Hence the dismal results of most foreign language programs. Why is this so?

Krashen draws a distinction between *language acquisition,* the subconscious process by which language is internalized, and *language learning,* which results in conscious knowledge of grammar and vocabulary. The latter can play a "monitor" or editing function when the learner is concerned about correctness, knows the rule, and has sufficient time to recall and apply it, for example, in the process of editing a written composition. But Krashen notes that, otherwise, these conditions are rarely met in real-life situations. The monitor is of limited usefulness when conversing with native speakers or even when ordering a meal in a foreign restaurant. As a result, students may perform well on written language tests without ever learning to use the language to com-

---

[14]Krashen (1985), p. 71.

[15]Edwards et al. (1984). This study won the Pimsleur Award, given by American Council on the Teaching of Foreign Languages for best published article of the year.

municate in practice. Nevertheless, conscious learning remains the method and goal of skill-building models. To the extent that students acquire any language at all in such classes, Krashen argues, comprehensible input—provided haphazardly rather than purposefully—is responsible.

The Comprehension Hypothesis has generated controversy. Alternative theories have been advanced, for example, stressing the importance of "comprehensible output" as a factor in second language acquisition and postulating a key role for student interaction with others.[16] Obviously, conversing with native speakers (assuming they are able to enunciate clearly and simply) can provide a rich source of comprehensible input. But we are unaware of any convincing evidence that languages are acquired through "practice." On the other hand, studies have shown that students can reach high levels of proficiency through input alone—that is, with little or no *production* of the language through speech or writing.[17]

Other critics are skeptical that a theory as simple and straightforward as Krashen's could account for such a complex phenomenon as language acquisition.[18] Advancing no particular theory of their own, some insist that explicit teaching of grammar, vocabulary, semantics, pragmatics, and even pronunciation is necessary because students in immersion classrooms sometimes have trouble with these features of the second language. Direct instruction, they say, is the only remedy. Such claims rely heavily on short-term studies in which older students—rarely K–12 English learners—are taught a linguistic form, such as word order, verb conjugation, relative clauses, and so forth, then tested on their conscious knowledge of the form soon after.[19] Their performance is then compared with that of language students who have not received the explicit lesson. Not surprisingly, the experimental groups tend to score higher than the

[16]Swain & Lapkin (1995).

[17]Krashen (2014).

[18]McLaughlin (1987).

[19]Saunders and Goldenberg (2010); this article favoring skill-building methods—published in a volume entitled *Improving Education for English Learners: Research Based Approaches*—concedes that the case for direct instruction actually lacks "strong, reliable findings" in research to support it, and is essentially a "best guess" (p. 60).

comparison groups (although exactly what type of instruction the latter have received, sheltered or otherwise, usually remains vague). But can students in the skill-building group still recall the form six months later?[20] Can they understand a sentence in which it appears? Can they use it themselves in speaking or writing? Such questions are left largely unanswered.

Back to Behaviorism

THESE STUDIES ARE PROBLEMATIC in additional ways that are beyond the scope of this book.[21] But it is noteworthy that, despite its lack of grounding in an elaborated theory, direct instruction relies heavily on behaviorist assumptions about how languages are acquired. Why is this significant? Because such assumptions were overthrown more than 50 years ago by the Chomskyan revolution in linguistics. They are premised on the notion that language is a finite set of responses to a finite set of stimuli, a collection of "speech habits" learned through imitation, repetition, and reinforcement. Yet, as Noam Chomsky pointed out, the number of possible sentences is infinite in any language; there is no limit to the grammatical combination of words. Behaviorism cannot explain how, after relatively limited exposure to a mother tongue, young children acquire complex syntactic structures and begin to produce "correct" utterances never heard before, by themselves or by others. What's more, they accomplish these amazing intellectual feats *without being explicitly taught.*

In Chomsky's theory, language is an innate cognitive capacity that is hard-wired into the human brain. He credits our *language acquisition device,* a mental "organ" that formulates grammatical rules from the linguistic input to which we are exposed. Absent a serious disability or complete social isolation, every one of us acquires at least one language. It is an unconscious and involuntary process, an essential part of being human. Understood in this way, language becomes a creative, open-ended activity rather than a closed system of behavioral habits.

[20] Some of these studies have shown a drop-off in accuracy in as little as four weeks; Krashen (2003), pp. 40–41.

[21] For a detailed response, see Krashen (2003), pp. 30–67.

Nevertheless, in the field of second and foreign language teaching, behaviorist pedagogy—i.e., direct instruction in various forms—maintains a large following, which seems to grow ever larger in this era of high-stakes testing. The connection is obvious. When educators' evaluations, pay, promotions, and job security depend on "metrics" of student performance, there is a natural tendency to teach to the test. Hence the proliferation of test-prep materials, paint-by-numbers teaching guides, and commercial learning systems, inevitably advertised as "research-based" and "aligned to the Common Core."

Which brings us back to SIOP. How closely does this brand of sheltered instruction conform to the theoretical basis for sheltering postulated by Stephen Krashen? How seriously should educators treat claims that SIOP has been "scientifically validated"? And most importantly, how beneficial—or nonbeneficial—is this model for English language learners?

2

What Is SIOP?

A CCORDING TO ITS CREATORS—Jana Echevarría, MaryEllen Vogt, and Deborah Short—SIOP was developed in the early 1990s to address what they saw as "a great deal of variability in both the design ... and the delivery" of sheltered instruction. "One sheltered classroom did not look like the next. ... In sum, there was no model for teachers to follow and few systematic and sustained forms of professional development."[22]

One could say the same, of course, about other program models for educating English language learners. Labels like *transitional bilingual education, developmental bilingual education,* and *two-way bilingual immersion* conceal wide variations in pedagogical methods, student and teacher characteristics, parent attitudes, and community concerns. But is that necessarily a problem? Why must there be a single, detailed "model" of each approach? And is there a basis in research for prescribing one? Naturally, educators of English learners should be well-versed in theories of second language acquisition and in methodologies such as sheltering and scaffolding. Their work should be informed by professional development and coaching from experienced colleagues on effective techniques in the classroom. But is there no room for diversity

[22]Echevarría et al. (2013), p. 15.

in teaching styles and techniques? Is there really *just one way* to shelter instruction?

SIOP's authors never explain the benefits of standardization; yet standardization was clearly their intent. They say they first conceived of SIOP "as a research and supervisory tool to determine if observed teachers incorporated key sheltered techniques consistently in their lessons." Later, as they refined a list of "effective classroom-based practices ... the protocol evolved into a lesson planning and delivery approach." What resulted was the SIOP® Model, incorporating "30 features grouped into eight main components." With federal funding through the Center for Research on Education, Diversity, and Excellence (CREDE), they conducted a study that rated teachers on their adherence to the protocol. According to Echevarría, Vogt, and Short, it "confirmed SIOP to be a valid and reliable measure of sheltered instruction." Additional support from the U.S. Department of Education and private foundations enabled them to conduct field tests, which reportedly found that "students who had teachers who implemented the SIOP with greater fidelity performed better than those who did not implement SIOP to a high degree."[23]

In other words, the authors decided that their first step would be to define sheltered instruction; research to evaluate their model's effectiveness would come later. Isn't this putting the cart before the horse? One would think that researchers concerned with program quality would have begun by conducting studies of various sheltering techniques and program designs to determine which were most promising in which contexts with which students. That kind of research might have led to some important advances in teaching English learners.[24]

Instead, the SIOP developers approached their project from the opposite direction. They began by announcing a model of sheltered instruction, incorporating a list of best practices that made sense to themselves and to a few colleagues. They presented this model as a detailed set of criteria, a rubric for effective sheltering. Then they asked a group of "raters" to evaluate the rubric for validity and reliability. Finally, they

[23]Echevarría et al. (2013), pp. 15–17

[24]Indeed, this emphasis was recommended by the National Research Council in an influential report; August & Hakuta (1997).

began conducting their own research on the model to see whether it worked. This is how SIOP came to be created and marketed commercially as "the only scientifically validated model of sheltered instruction."

We have several questions about this process. Let's take them one by one.

Valid and Reliable?

FIRST, IS IT ACCURATE to call SIOP a form of sheltered instruction? Does the SIOP rubric provide a valid and reliable measure of whether teachers are effectively sheltering a lesson for English learners? This claim relies on a study published in 2001, in which "four teachers experienced in SI" were asked to rate other teachers by watching six 45-minute videos. Three of the videos showed lessons that the researchers believed to be "highly representative" of sheltered instruction; three were deemed not representative. When polled, the raters generally agreed that the first group of teachers scored higher on the SIOP rubric—in other words, that they used more of "the 30 features grouped into eight main components"—than the second group. Ergo, the study's authors concluded, SIOP was confirmed to be "an invaluable tool for both preservice and in-service teachers to assess their implementation of effective sheltered instruction."[25]

That's it? Yes, that's it—the entire foundation for the claim that SIOP equals sheltered instruction. A tiny study in which an unidentified group validates this conclusion. Who were the raters? Were they randomly selected or (as seems more likely) colleagues of the SIOP authors? What does it mean that they were "experienced in SI"? Three were reported to have "doctorates in education," but did that necessarily make them authorities in effective sheltering techniques? Were they already familiar with SIOP? Or were they perhaps among the practitioners who reportedly helped to develop the model? If so, wouldn't that create a bias? And what about the teachers they evaluated? How extensive was their experience in working with English learners? Did one group receive training in SIOP methods while the other did not?

More broadly: What, if any, theory of second language acquisition was

[25]Guarino et al. (2001).

used in defining sheltered instruction? Were alternative theories considered, debated, included, or rejected?

None of these questions are answered in the paper. Yet they go to the heart of the issue of *construct validity*—that is, whether a test accurately measures the characteristic that it purports to measure. They are also relevant to *reliability,* the likelihood that results of a test will be consistent, no matter who happens to take or administer it.

In this case, we are given no explanation of how or why SIOP equals sheltered instruction, other than the opinion of a small, poorly identified group. We are essentially being asked to trust the experts, whoever they might be. This study is a classic case of circular reasoning. *All it really seems to prove is that if you assemble a number of like-minded people, who share a certain view of sheltering and how it should be done, a test will confirm that they agree with each other most of the time about what sheltering means.* Thus the article's elaborate data tables showing how consistently they agree become irrelevant to issues of validity and reliability.

Best Practices or Worst?

ON CLOSE INSPECTION, a majority of SIOP's 30 features are generic best practices—bits of conventional wisdom about "what works" for all students. Rather than targeting the particular needs of English learners, they could be applied to virtually any K–12 classroom. Several features are simply common-sense principles that most experienced educators would endorse, including #3, *Content concepts appropriate for age and educational background of students;* #8, *Links explicitly made between past learning and new concepts;* and #26, *Pacing of the lesson appropriate to students' skill levels.* Others are familiar practices in contemporary teaching, such as #4, *Supplementary materials used to a high degree, making the lesson clear and meaningful;* #15, *A variety of questions or tasks that promote higher-order thinking skills;* and #16, *Frequent opportunities for interaction and discussion.* It is curious that such features of "good teaching," which have nothing directly to do with sheltered instruction, make up much of a rubric for defining it.

More serious problems crop up in the features that do relate specifically to English learners. Some are compatible with the Comprehension Hypothesis, the theoretical basis for sheltering outlined above; others are incompatible. Several of the latter stress direct instruction and thus imply a view of language acquisition sometimes described as the Skill-Building Hypothesis. As Stephen Krashen points out in a recent article, SIOP ignores the fundamental conflict between the two theories; it tries to incorporate both. "According to the Comprehension Hypothesis," Krashen explains, "our knowledge of grammar and vocabulary emerges as a result of getting comprehensible input"—for example, through sheltered subject matter instruction. "According to the Skill-Building Hypothesis, we first learn grammar and vocabulary, but can only use them after they are made automatic. ... Skill-Building thus depends on conscious learning, output, and correction. In contrast, the Comprehension Hypothesis claims that we acquire language and develop literacy in only one way: when we understand messages; that is, when we understand what we hear and what we read."[26]

This contrast has major implications for teaching. One approach stresses techniques for making input comprehensible through simplified speech, clear explanations, links to background knowledge, and the use of modeling and manipulatives—in other words, the sheltering of academic content to foster language acquisition. The other approach calls for an explicit focus on language form, "preteaching" vocabulary before each lesson, lots of "language practice opportunities," and correction of grammatical errors. SIOP not only combines all of these contradictory features; it requires that teachers ultimately learn to use all of them in each lesson.

This theoretical muddle also creates a quandary for evaluating SIOP research. If the model is faithfully applied and proves effective (or not), who can say why? When diametrically opposed methods are combined, it becomes impossible to account for a model's success or failure. Imagine a nutrition study that evaluated the effects of a high-fiber, high-carbohydrate, high-saturated-fat diet simultaneously; the results would never be conclusive. Not surprisingly, the research findings on SIOP remain cloudy as well.

[26]Krashen (2013), p. 11.

3

'Research-Based' Hype

BOTH PEARSON EDUCATION AND THE NONPROFIT Center for Applied Linguistics (CAL) have promoted SIOP as an all-purpose educational product: a tool for evaluating teachers, a template for lesson planning and "delivery," and a course of professional development. They advertise their model as ideal not only for English learners (pre-K–12 and adult), but also for mainstream and special education students in the United States, as well as language students worldwide. Clearly, they believe the market potential is vast.

Pearson's SIOP website offers no fewer than 15 SIOP® Model books, "a ground-breaking series ... trusted by more than 600,000 educators." It also features SIOP® Institutes (two days on-site: $700 to $750; one day online: $250), along with conferences, district trainings, trainer-of-trainer workshops, research and diagnostic services, videos, webinars, case studies, and classroom activities. Other hot items include the SIOP® for Teachers Virtual Institute, the SIOP® Inter-Rater Reliability institute, and related online courses. Pearson claims:

> [E]mpirically-validated research indicates that The SIOP® Model works for teachers of all students—especially ELs. When implemented to a high degree, SIOP® is proven to:
> • Increase student achievement

- Improve academic content skills and language skills
- Deliver results aligned to district objectives
- Prepare students to become college and career ready[27]

For its part, the Center for Applied Linguistics describes SIOP as "a unifying professional development framework ... a school-wide intervention ... because of its applicability across content areas and its established research base." It, too, advertises a full product line, including SIOP Institutes and workshops, a SIOP Comprehensive Package ($425), Starter Package ($285), Professional Development Manual ($205), videos, lesson plans, and other publications, as well as consulting services and site visits. According to CAL's ad copy, "the SIOP Model can be used by professionals from a wide range of backgrounds"—including teachers in elementary or secondary schools, preservice or inservice, bilingual or English as a second language (ESL) or two-way immersion, as well as coaches and staff developers, school district administrators, and teacher education faculty—with full confidence that SIOP is "research-based and validated."[28] And don't forget early childhood and adult education, as well as GED programs, the latest markets that CAL seeks to penetrate. Is there any group of students for whom SIOP would not be recommended? Setting aside the financial motives, it must be asked: Why is SIOP needed or even appropriate in all of these diverse contexts? What educational purposes does it serve? These questions remain unanswered.

By now there are several published studies purporting to prove the SIOP model's effectiveness with elementary and secondary students. But, as mentioned earlier, the federal Institute of Education Sciences reviewed these studies and found all of them lacking—that is, none could "establish that the comparison group was comparable to the intervention group prior to the start of the intervention."[29] In other words, any advantage claimed for SIOP versus non-SIOP methods may or may not have had anything to do with the educational approach. Without valid comparison groups, it is impossible to say. Therefore, the SIOP studies provide *no scientific evidence one way or another*, IES concluded. And

[27] Pearson (n.d.b).
[28] Center for Applied Linguistics (n.d.a).
[29] Institute of Education Sciences (2013), p. 1.

yet, the "research-based" advertisements from Pearson and CAL have continued virtually without challenge. Not a single independent researcher, it seems, has closely and critically examined the studies' findings—at least, not until the 2013 article by Stephen Krashen.

Among the published articles on SIOP, Krashen could locate only five that provided comparative evidence regarding the model's effectiveness, all but one authored by SIOP developers themselves. Of the five studies, three lacked statistical significance; *that is, the data observed may have reflected nothing more than random variation.* In some cases, important information was missing, such as statistical means, standard deviations, and characteristics of students and teachers. When SIOP was compared to non-SIOP approaches, the "effect sizes"—observed differences in student achievement between the two groups—were usually small.

What follows is a summary of these studies, informed by Krashen's analyses.

Fidelity Study

ECHEVARRÍA AND COLLEAGUES rated 12 middle school teachers—eight with SIOP training and four without—on a biweekly basis using the SIOP rubric.[30] A total of 1,021 students, randomly assigned to each group of teachers, were tested before and after four science units using multiple-choice and fill-in-the-blanks questions. While the study took place in a "large urban school district with high numbers of ELs," the percentage of English learners included in the research was unspecified. Nor were results disaggregated for teachers in the experimental and comparison groups. Apparently the range of test scores was about the same for both groups, even though teachers in the former received "intensive" SIOP training and coaching (help with lesson plans, classroom observations, and "debriefing"), while teachers in the latter did not.

The authors reported that "overall the teachers who implemented the model with the greatest degree of fidelity (i.e., had the highest scores) also had students who made the greatest gains. ... As our study shows, there is a direct relationship between level of implementation [of SIOP] and student achievement" (pp. 431–433). The reported strength of this

[30]Echevarría et al. (2011a).

relationship (r^2) was .2183. Thus, as Krashen explains, "knowing a teacher's score gives us about 22% of the information we need to predict the gain their students made." However, *the results do not reach statistical significance*—a matter left unmentioned by the paper's authors. "It also needs to be pointed out that a correlation using a sample size of only 12 is not 'powerful' enough to detect significant differences," Krashen adds.[31]

Science Study

USING THE SAME SUBJECTS included in the Fidelity Study, the researchers again tested 1,021 students who had been randomly assigned to 12 teachers.[32] Eight of the teachers had received 2.5 days of SIOP training, plus intensive coaching and feedback, while four had received no SIOP training, coaching, or feedback. Unlike the earlier study, this one disaggregated the students by language proficiency: 217 English learners (21%), 442 former English learners (44%), and 352 native-English speakers (35%).[33]

Tests were administered before and after each eight-week unit, and students in all language categories made modest gains. While those in the SIOP classrooms did slightly better, once again the differences between intervention and comparison groups were not statistically significant, as the authors conceded. "However," they added, "effect sizes [of the SIOP treatment] ranged from .103 to .197 for the nonessay and essay components of the posttest respectively" (p. 347). This wording implies that the outcomes were somehow encouraging for SIOP. In fact, even if the effect sizes had reached statistical significance, they would still be minimal.[34] For the English learners tested, Krashen calculated even smaller effect sizes of .062 and .087, respectively.

Trying to put another positive spin on the results, the authors argued that "given the short duration of the professional development and the intervention period itself, the effect sizes give some room for optimism.

[31] Krashen (2013), p. 15.
[32] Echevarría et al. (2011b).
[33] However, the totals in Table 1 of the article add do not add up to 1,021, as reported.
[34] Krashen (2013, p. 17) notes that an effect size of Cohen's $d = .2$ is generally considered small, "equivalent to a correlation of $r = .1$ and $r^2 = .01$, which means that it accounts for about 1% of the variability." A medium effect size is $d = .5$; a large effect size, $d = .8$.

It is quite possible that given more exposure to high-quality SIOP science instruction, the students would have performed better" (p. 348). Of course, they might also have performed worse; the study offers no basis for predicting.

"Perhaps most importantly," the researchers noted, "the level of SIOP Model implementation was not optimal." They suggested that some teachers, even though they had volunteered to take part in the research, became reluctant participants, thus "undermin[ing] treatment impact" and "limit[ing] the power" of the study (p. 348). There is no indication, however, that any of the teachers were interviewed about their lack of enthusiasm for SIOP. The researchers apparently regarded their model as a finished product rather than a work in progress that might benefit from criticism by practitioners.

Finally, the authors emphasized—as an "important finding"—that "there was no evidence to suggest that students who were English Only students were negatively impacted by having a teacher who was delivering SIOP-based instruction. ... The performance of all student groups improved on average, which shows that although initially designed for English learners, the SIOP Model can benefit EO students as well" (p. 348). *Really?* Did the study explore whether native-English speakers might have performed better in a well-implemented program that was not tailored specifically for English learners? Of course not. Yet this "finding"—that SIOP works for just about any student—is being widely used in marketing the model.

While SIOP-taught students in each language category may have shown greater gains than their counterparts in the comparison group, it is impossible to say by how much, since the article failed to disaggregate the pretest baseline scores. All we are told is that "these implementation results are at least promising, as are the estimates of effect sizes" (p. 348). Bear in mind that the results were not statistically significant; from a social-science research perspective, they "promise" nothing.

We have to wonder whether an impartial team of researchers, with no professional or financial stake in the outcome, would have drawn the same conclusions on the basis of such weak data. Viewed objectively, this study's results were inconclusive regarding the effectiveness of SIOP. You wouldn't learn that, however, by reading the glowing accounts of the research by Pearson Education and the Center for Applied Linguistics.

Writing Study

IN 1998–2000, DURING EARLY WORK on the SIOP model, the developers conducted research to test its impact on student writing skills.[35] The study included 458 English learners in grades 6–8 at eight urban schools on the East and West coasts; 23 teachers participated, 19 in the experimental group and four in the comparison group. According to the SIOP authors, the two groups had similar teaching experience, but their levels of support differed substantially during the study. Teachers in the experimental group spent up to two years "learning and practicing the SIOP model through an extensive professional development process." In addition,

> [t]he project teachers and researchers formed a learning community to refine the model through an examination of the teachers' classroom practices and student response to the SIOP lessons. On both coasts teachers participated in 3-day staff development institutes on the SIOP model each summer and in several reunion meetings during each school year. ... Teachers discussed student reaction to SIOP lesson methods and shared samples of student work. Between meetings, teachers and researchers communicated via a closed electronic list. [p. 203]

Teachers in the comparison group enjoyed none of these advantages. Nor were they reported to receive any other form of professional development during the study. So one might reasonably expect that their students were at a *dis*advantage when tested; indeed, progress was limited for these children, judging from the pretest and posttest data reported. On the IMAGE[36] writing assessment, English learners in the SIOP classrooms outpaced those in the non-SIOP classrooms, and the differences were judged to be statistically significant overall.[37] But how big an impact was detected? Using a rather technical formula, the authors reported the following result:

[35] Echevarría et al. (2006).

[36] Illinois Measure of Annual Growth in English.

[37] While there were five subtests of student writing, the differences between students in the experimental and comparison groups were statistically significant in just three.

The effect size of the intervention calculated for the intervention group as $d = M_1 - M_2/\sigma_{pooled}$ with M_1 = posttest total writing and M_2 = pretest total writing scores, was +.833. That effect size is considered large by most indexes. ... [p. 205]

Quite impressive, or so it would seem. There was just one problem. The effect size was not calculated in the usual way, that is, in relation to the comparison group; it simply involved gains made by the SIOP-taught group during the two years. This is unacceptable in controlled scientific studies. One normally expects a group of students, on average, to have learned *something* between pretest and posttest, regardless of the educational treatment. The key questions are: Would they have learned more (or less) in an alternative program? And how substantial were the differences—in other words, what was the *comparative effect size?* By focusing on the SIOP group alone, the article avoided addressing these issues. Worse, it created an exaggerated impression of SIOP's impact for readers who lack expertise in statistics and mathematical notation; one might even call this deceptive.[38]

Krashen did the orthodox calculation, analyzing the difference in gains between the SIOP and non-SIOP students, and found an effect size of .21, weighted by sample size. In other words, SIOP had at best a small impact on writing achievement in this study, even if you discount the serious comparability issues, such as the comparison group's apparent lack of any professional development in how to serve English learners.

New Jersey Study

THE MOST RECENT PUBLISHED RESEARCH on SIOP focused on the development of academic literacy among English learners in two New Jersey districts.[39] This was a "quasi-experimental" study, that is, a study whose design relied on matching student and school characteristics (diversity, size, socioeconomic status, etc.) rather than on random assignment of research subjects to the intervention and comparison groups. The researchers compared student achievement in middle-school and high-school classrooms taught by SIOP-trained versus non-SIOP trained

---

[38]We thank Stephen Krashen for bringing this problem to our attention.
[39]Short et al. (2012).

teachers. The comparisons involved 267 English learners in the SIOP classrooms and 168 in the non-SIOP classrooms, who were assessed in reading, writing, and oral language using the IDEA Language Proficiency Tests (IPT).

By the second year of the study, the researchers reported superior outcomes for students in the SIOP-taught classrooms on all measures. But again the observed differences were small, with an overall effect size of .23 for total English. There were statistically significant differences in writing (.31) and oral language (.29), but only a slight, nonsignificant edge in reading (.16).[40] The study's authors explained these less than impressive outcomes by asserting that "in general, effect sizes for treatment differences tend to be greatest in the primary grades, with a steady decline as the grades progress." Still, they concluded that "implementation of the SIOP model had a positive effect on the development of English language proficiency" (p. 353).

As in other SIOP studies, questions remain about exactly what the researchers were comparing. No information was provided about the educational program in the comparison district, except that it was labeled "ESL." Even more problematic was the fact that teachers were not randomly selected; rather, they were "recruited" to participate in the study, a potential source of bias. Very little information was provided about the professional backgrounds of the non-SIOP-trained teachers or about their classroom methods. But few seem to have had certifications or Master's degrees in ESL or related fields (versus about a third of their SIOP-trained counterparts). While the SIOP teachers received extensive training and support from the research team over a two-year period, teachers in the comparison group merely "participated in regular district professional development days for 2 to 3 days each year," the content of which was unspecified. In addition, two ESL teachers in the comparison group had training in using a new textbook and a language proficiency assessment, and they "led a 1-hour workshop on student diversity and accommodations for ELLs" (p. 346). If the comparison dis-

[40]No longitudinal analyses charting the progress of individual students were possible, the authors said, because only a small number were tested for consecutive years.

trict had had a coherent pedagogical approach for teaching English learners, the professional development picture would look quite different. Short et al. conceded that those "who agreed to participate in the SIOP training may have been different from the teachers who did not, and the differences may have affected the [student] outcomes" (p. 356). Put another way, the non-SIOP group appears to have had considerably less training, guidance, or interest in teaching English learners. So even the small advantages reported for the SIOP group may be exaggerated.

Reading Study

ONLY ONE COMPARATIVE STUDY OF SIOP has been published by anyone other than the SIOP developers themselves. McIntyre and colleagues compared reading scores for students in SIOP classrooms against those in non-SIOP classrooms.[41] The researchers sponsored an intensive, 18-month professional development project involving 23 teachers of elementary English learners in an urban school district in the Midwest. After the teachers were judged on their adherence to the SIOP model, the students of only seven "full implementers"—that is, teachers with perfect scores on the SIOP rubric—were included in the final analysis. The reading performance of these 50 English learners were then compared to that of 50 peers from a "demographically matched sample of students in classrooms of teachers who had not participated in the professional development."

It would be hard to conceive a research design that stacked the cards more advantageously for SIOP, comparing a group of intensively trained teachers with a group that had no reported training in working with English learners. And yet, the edge for SIOP in student growth in reading was very small[42] and the differences were not statistically significant. As in the other studies reviewed above, the authors advanced various explanations for why the SIOP results were below their expectations—in this case, small sample size and uncontrolled "dissimilarities" between the intervention and comparison groups. In the end, they conceded:

[41]McIntyre et al. (2010).
[42]Although none was reported in the article, after analyzing the data Krashen calculated an effect size of .16.

It is impossible to tease out all confounding variables of the research to make definite claims about the SIOP model. ... This study illustrates that *the SIOP model at least does not appear detrimental to reading achievement* and may even support it, if it is fully implemented as intended by the model authors. [p. 348; emphasis added]

Well, that's comforting. A growing body of research suggests that SIOP may not be harmful to English learners and might even be helpful if teachers could only get it right. McIntyre et al. failed to consider another possibility: that these students might have learned more in a well-designed, alternative model of instruction. *But SIOP has yet to face such fair competition in any of the studies conducted thus far.* Indeed, it appears that none of the comparison students were provided with a clearly defined program for English learners or with teachers who were trained to implement one.

Bottom Line

A MAJOR LIMITATION OF ALL THE SIOP RESEARCH to date is that teachers are rated on their faithful compliance with all 30 features of the model. That might be meaningful if SIOP reflected a clear philosophy of sheltered instruction. Instead, as Krashen notes, it combines diametrically opposed approaches (along with various "best practices" not specific to teaching English learners). So the researchers had no way to determine the impact on student achievement of teachers applying methodologies consistent with the Comprehension Hypothesis versus those consistent with the Skill Building Hypothesis.

Ultimately, what do the SIOP research findings add up to? First, as Krashen points out, "the results are only modest, despite a large investment in SIOP training."[43] Second, the "unusual number of flaws and gaps in the [SIOP] studies"—including unknown factors, such as the percentage of English learners in the classrooms being studied, and known factors likely to bias results in favor of SIOP, such as teachers volunteering or being specially selected for the study—"make the empirical results

---

[43] An academic supporter of SIOP, who regards it as "a useful and coherent instructional model," does not disagree: "SIOP ... has yet to demonstrate more than a very modest effect on student learning"; Goldenberg (2013), p.7.

even less impressive." Finally, "even if SIOP were shown to be successful, because SIOP is a mixed bag we would not know what is responsible for the results because the effect of different parts of SIOP was not separately analyzed."[44]

We agree with Krashen and with the federal Institute of Education Sciences, which notes the lack of comparable control groups in the SIOP studies conducted to date.[45] Viewed in its entirety, all that this research has demonstrated is that a lot of professional development and coaching in educating English learners may yield slightly better student outcomes than little or no professional development and coaching. If such a finding can justify the label "scientifically validated," the standard of effectiveness is very low indeed.

[44]Krashen (2013), p. 20.

[45]In a Pearson-produced video, Jana Echevarría claims otherwise: "Overall, we found that teachers who use the SIOP Model, their students outperform students whose teachers don't use the SIOP Model, in other words, students who are in the control classes. *[The teachers] use the same materials, the same curriculum, more or less the same pacing,* yet the difference in the two groups is that one group of teachers uses the SIOP Model techniques and strategies in their lesson delivery"; Pearson (2013; emphasis added). The implication here, that the treatment and comparison groups differed only in the teaching methods used, is not supported in any of the published studies on SIOP thus far, including papers coauthored by Echevarría herself.

4

SIOP in Theory: Teaching by Numbers

E SPECIALLY FOR BEGINNERS, A PAINT-BY-NUMBERS KIT can produce results superior to freehand artwork. If you follow instructions, color within the lines, and avoid improvising, just about anyone can replicate a prepackaged "masterpiece." It's simple and virtually risk-free, with no need to engage in creative art or self-expression or critical judgment. In fact, it's best to avoid adventurous impulses and stick to the outline. Otherwise the work gets challenging and the outcome unpredictable.

SIOP works in a similar way. It offers extensive guidance that teachers inexperienced with English learners sometimes find appealing. It specifies "30 features grouped into eight main components" that serve as an all-encompassing model for lesson planning, classroom instruction and assessment, professional development, and teacher evaluation. Rather than handing teachers a prewritten script for each lesson, SIOP *coaches them* on how to create a prewritten script for each lesson. The directions are highly detailed. "Language objectives" and "content objectives" are not only mapped out in advance. They must also be "clearly defined, displayed, and reviewed with students,"[46] so there is no confusion about (or distraction from) the expected learning outcomes. These rules apply to SIOP classrooms as early as kindergarten. An extensive list of teaching

[46]SIOP Features 1 and 2; Echevarría et al. (2013), pp. 26–37.

techniques is also prescribed: "supplementary materials used ... links explicitly made [to] past learning ... key vocabulary emphasized ... ample opportunities for students to use learning strategies ... wait time for student responses ... grouping configurations ... activities [that] integrate all language skills (i.e., reading, writing, thinking, and speaking)"—to name just a few.[47] Meanwhile, assessments of student learning, "directly linked to ... language and content objectives," are applied throughout the lesson.[48] Nothing is left to chance.

SIOP's developers insist:

> [This] is not, however, a step-by-step approach. Instead, it accommodates variation in teaching style. Teachers may accomplish their language and content learning goals in ways suited to the particular lesson, asking students to, for example, hypothesize the results of a science experiment with peers using cause-effect sentences, argue a position on the use of taxation to reduce a deficit, or write a journal entry about a text-to-self connection after reading a short story.[49]

Apparently, they believe these "variations" are examples of imaginative and engaging strategies (students might not agree). The problem is that when a program model requires teachers to incorporate 30 specific elements into each lesson,[50] it leaves little leeway for spontaneity, much less for creative approaches or teachable moments. Nor is there any room for students to pursue their own interests or help to direct their own learning.

From start to finish—beginning with the posting of language and content objectives on the board and ending with the "critically important ... final review"[51] of how those objectives have been mastered—SIOP is

[47]Echevarría et al. (2013), pp. 288–294.
[48]Echevarría et al. (2013), p. 235.
[49]Short et al. (2012), p. 337.
[50]The SIOP authors are contradictory on this point. Sometimes they suggest that the 30 Features may be incorporated over a period of several days. But in an "FAQ," they respond to the question as follows: "Do I have to incorporate all thirty SIOP features in every lesson? Eventually, yes. We recommend that elementary teachers begin implementing one component at a time in one subject area, until all components are implemented in that subject area. The ultimate goal is to add other subjects until all are 'SIOPized'"; Echevarría et al. (2013), p. 283.
[51]Echevarría et al. (2013), p. 219.

teacher-centric, a classic transmission model. Sadly, this approach is all too common in the education of low-income and minority students and of English learners in particular: *Learning is conceived not as something a learner does, but as something that is done to a learner.*[52]

No doubt the creators of SIOP would disagree with this characterization. Sprinkled throughout their model are bite-sized morsels of progressive teaching, such as cooperative learning, scaffolding techniques, and interactive games, along with popular strategies including Think-Pair-Share. Yet such ingredients can be combined in various ways. What matters is how the overall recipe comes together. In other words, what is the educational approach that guides instruction in a coherent way? In SIOP's case, the approach is contradictory. While the model is flavored with some progressive tidbits, it largely consists of controlled activities, explicit instruction in language mechanics, and predetermined outcomes. Stir it all together and you get a pedagogical mishmash.

At least, that's what SIOP looks like on the surface. The reality is worse.

Philosophical Muddle

JUST AS SIOP COMBINES DISPARATE METHODOLOGIES and strategies, it mixes elements of educational philosophies ranging from behaviorism to constructivism. As one of the SIOP authors explains:

> [E]ffective teachers typically use a balanced approach that includes choices rooted in different learning theories. Many instructional methods and practices make use of aspects of several theoretical approaches. Similarly, sheltered instruction is not driven by a single theory, but rather exhibits influences of several theoretical perspectives.[53]

Indeed, the SIOP manuals and sample lessons recommend a hodgepodge of approaches—whatever seems to "work"—rather than advancing a clear rationale for how to teach English learners. But let's leave aside for the moment the question of whether SIOP's promiscuous approach to theory is a good idea.

[52]Reversing a wise formulation by Falk (2009): "Learning is something that a learner does, not something that is done to a learner" (p. 26).
[53]Echevarria & Graves (2003), p. 35.

The immediate question is how SIOP could achieve "balance" between pedagogical theories that clash in almost every respect. Constructivism, for example, starts with the premise that deep (as opposed to rote) learning is an internally driven process of *making meaning* from experience. The constructivist teacher plans a logical sequence of activities, but avoids guiding students toward one "correct" answer or toward a predetermined skill-set. Her goal is to assist them in thinking independently, critically, and creatively—that is, to foster active rather than passive learning. For the behaviorist educator, by contrast, students' mental processes are considered unimportant. What matters are external, measurable results achieved through positive or negative reinforcement. Relying primarily on memorization, repetition, testing, and rewards or punishments, he seeks to modify student behavior—by instilling a body of academic material chosen by external authorities.

Given these stark differences, how is it possible to build a pedagogical model that features both approaches simultaneously? We can think of only one way: by distorting one of the educational philosophies to make it compatible with the other. This is precisely what SIOP does.

Take the concept of scaffolding, a key element of constructivist teaching. It refers to various forms of support that prepare learners to perform at higher levels than they could reach on their own. For scaffolding to work successfully, the task should be just beyond a student's current abilities—not too easy and not too difficult—in what Vygotsky called the *zone of proximal development.* In practice, scaffolding might mean asking probing questions, offering feedback, making connections, fostering interactions, differentiating instruction for individual learners, drawing on background knowledge, or modeling a difficult process. The goal is to make the curriculum accessible while encouraging exploration and discovery, providing just enough support to keep students progressing until they can climb higher independently.

SIOP incorporates what it calls scaffolding (Feature 14), but in a very different way. The techniques recommended—including small-group instruction, partnering students for activities, peer tutoring, think-alouds, one-on-one coaching, guided practice, and use of graphic organizers—can be found in a variety of settings, including constructivist classrooms.

For SIOP's purposes, however, scaffolding is provided in a tightly structured format. After "explicitly teaching a concept," teachers lead students in "practicing" what has been taught, then divide them into groups for more repetition, with continual supervision and "re-teaching" until they are finally judged "successful." This regimented process is far from the open-ended use of scaffolding that Vygotsky had in mind. It's much closer to Madeline Hunter's ITIP[54] Model for Direct Instruction, an openly behaviorist approach whose seven-step format closely resembles SIOP's eight components.[55] Scaffolding is applied in this context, not to engage students through authentic and meaningful activities, but to transmit a designated set of skills and knowledge. It becomes simply another way to exert control over a lesson, to prevent any deviation from language and content objectives. A more accurate term would be "straitjacketing."

Corrupting Krashen

SIOP's VERSION OF SHELTERING is equally distorted. Bear in mind that the concept and terminology of *sheltered instruction* originated with Stephen Krashen more than a decade before SIOP was introduced. As a theoretically grounded methodology, it has exerted a major influence on the education of second language learners, not only in the United States, but in many other countries as well. Yet, curiously, the SIOP authors fail to credit Krashen for his breakthrough in any edition of their manual, *Making Content Comprehensible for English Learners.* They also ignore studies on sheltered instruction other than their own[56]—as if they were the only researchers in this area. Were these omissions related to their queasiness about the trademarking of a "model" derived from Krashen's work without his knowledge or consent?[57] Appropriating the original

[54]Instructional Theory into Practice

[55]Ellis (2005); Madeline Cheek Hunter (1916–1994).

[56]E.g., reviews of the literature such as Krashen (1991) and Dupuy (2000).

[57]According to the U.S. Patent and Trademark Office, the trademark for Sheltered Instruction Observation Protocol (SIOP®) was registered on September 7, 2004, by the SIOP Institute, a California Limited Liability Company whose principal officers were Jana Echevarría and MaryEllen Vogt. That same year the trademark and the SIOP Institute were acquired by Pearson, which now claims "exclusive ownership" of both; Pearson (n.d.c). We asked Stephen Krashen whether he had ever considered applying for a trademark on sheltered instruction. His response: "It never occurred to me, just as it never occurred to me to patent the Monitor Hypothesis or Comprehensible Input."

ideas of others is not unheard of, especially when large corporations are involved, but it raises obvious ethical concerns. In addition, the SIOP authors may have sought to distance themselves from the controversy that Krashen's Comprehension Hypothesis has stirred in some quarters. Or perhaps they just wanted to avoid a discussion about the differences between SIOP and the original concept of sheltered instruction. Those differences are what most concern us here, and they are significant.

As noted previously, SIOP is theoretically eclectic. It incorporates elements of two diametrically opposed views of second language acquisition. By contrast, Krashen's concept of sheltered instruction is theoretically based. That is, it

> derives from one important concept: Subject matter teaching in a second language, when it is comprehensible, is language teaching, because it provides comprehensible input. ... [T]he focus of the class is on subject matter, not language. This encourages a focus on meaning, not form, and results in more comprehensible input, and thus more language acquisition. Sheltered subject matter classes are thus not "ESL Math" or "ESL History" but are "math" and "history."[58]

Yet SIOP, without advancing any explanation, puts "language objectives" on a par with "content objectives" and teaches both explicitly. While the authors emphasize comprehensible input as one of SIOP's "components"—this time they do cite Krashen[59]—they also stress direct instruction in grammar, vocabulary, and even pronunciation, along with correction of linguistic errors.

This tendency is illustrated in sample lessons provided by the SIOP authors, which tend to focus primarily on language at the expense of content, to stress the medium and not the message. Take, for example, a hypothetical teacher identified as a "high implementer" of SIOP, as he introduces a unit on "The Rain Forest." "Mr. Montoya" begins by distributing a magazine article and giving his 7th grade class one minute to preview the text. He divides students into pairs to make predictions about what the text will say, then writes their predictions on chart paper, counting "votes" for the most popular items. Next he reads aloud the

---

[58]Krashen (1991), p. 183.
[59]Nevertheless, they misconstrue Krashen's concept, as noted in Chapter 5 below.

first four paragraphs of the article, with students following along, to see how the predictions turned out. The results are posted on the chart and additional predictions are added based on the text so far. Students are then instructed to read the next section of the article and to pick out two or three important vocabulary words. Again votes are taken, in order to select the ten most important words to write on the board. Students check their predictions against the article and use sticky notes to indicate where in the text their questions are answered. Then they write summary sentences about the article using the key vocabulary words. Finally, Mr. Montoya asks a few factual questions about the article and tells the students to write a letter, from the point of view of the President of the United States, appealing to lumber companies to save the rainforest.[60]

For a subject with so much potential to stimulate the imagination, it's hard to imagine a more tedious approach, practically guaranteed to deaden the enthusiasm of 12-year-olds. Rather than inspire students to explore the exotic creatures and cultures of the Amazon, this "exemplary" SIOP teacher builds his lesson on word lists and text analysis. Before being allowed to read about the rainforest, students are repeatedly exhorted to make predictions about what the text will say and to cast votes prioritizing items of vocabulary. Who wouldn't be bored? One can imagine the spitballs that fly whenever Mr. Montoya turns his back.

The problem is compounded for English learners, who are likely to tune out not only the content but the language input as well. Not at all what Krashen intended. He conceived sheltered instruction as a way of teaching language incidentally and naturally, while students' minds are engaged by subjects that interest them. According to the Monitor Hypothesis, a focus on form does not contribute to real language acquisition. It results in consciously learned knowledge of language, which makes a small contribution to accuracy, and only in limited situations, such as when editing written text.

There are several other points of conflict. First is Krashen's insistence that a sheltered classroom consists of second language learners only. As in the successful French immersion approach, no native speakers are included. "When all students are in the same linguistic boat," he explains,

[60]Echevarría et al. (2013), pp. 134–137.

"it is easier for the teacher to make the input comprehensible."[61] Conversely, it is much harder for the teacher to present challenging, grade-appropriate content while meeting all the needs of students who vary widely in language proficiency. If Canada's French immersion programs had practiced this kind of heterogeneous grouping, it's unlikely they would have been so successful or influential. Instead, they enabled teachers to master the art and science of making instruction comprehensible by assigning them students at roughly the same level of French.[62]

Second, by Krashen's definition, "sheltered classes are for intermediate [language learners], not beginners." The reason should be obvious: "It is extremely difficult to teach subject matter to those who have acquired none or little of the language. Beginners should be in regular ESL, where they are assured of comprehensible input."[63] Unrealistic language demands create, in effect, a sink-or-swim situation, in which academic learning is minimal.

Third, the Comprehension Hypothesis, on which Krashen's concept of sheltering is based, holds that *input* is what matters in second language acquisition—not *output*. As noted above, forcing students to "produce" a second language can be counterproductive. Output per se does not contribute directly to language acquisition, and forcing speech before students have acquired enough language to express their meaning tends to create anxiety and embarrassment, thereby raising the "affective filter" that keeps input from getting through.

Without addressing any of these issues, SIOP's authors designate their model as appropriate for English learners of all proficiency levels, including newcomer students and others just beginning to acquire the language. Mr. Montoya's class, for example, included both native-English speakers and English learners of "mixed proficiency levels." In addition, SIOP Feature 21 requires *activities that integrate all language skills (reading, writing, listening, speaking)*—that is, forced output in English for all students, beginning at the earliest stages of acquiring the language.

[61]Krashen (1991), p. 183.

[62]One caveat: In these "one-way" programs, native-like French input came almost entirely from the teacher. "Two-way" immersion, when it features true collaborative learning among students acquiring each others' languages, represents an exception to this rule (a point discussed further in Chapter 5).

[63]Krashen (2001), p. 112.

Dumbing It Down

COULD SUCH A ONE-SIZE-FITS-ALL MODEL be effective in serving students with diverse needs? How does SIOP deal with the comprehensibility problem? Obviously, there are two options: "dumb down" the curriculum to a level that all English learners can handle or teach academic content at a level that leaves many English learners behind. The requirements of SIOP often steer teachers toward the first option, although it doesn't always succeed in making lessons comprehensible, especially in mainstream classrooms.

Mary Ann Zehr, an *Education Week* reporter, spent a day observing SIOP-trained teachers in Clifton, N.J., the "treatment" district in the New Jersey study discussed in Chapter 3. Here is her description of how the model works for students at differing levels of English:

> One of the SIOP methods that [Michele Trigo, a middle-school math teacher] has found particularly effective is having students say at the end of the lesson a sentence beginning with any of the following expressions: "I think," "I know," "I learned," or "I wonder." After a recent lesson on circles and circumferences, she asked each student to do that exercise.
>
> "I learned that to find the radius, you have to divide the diameter by 2," said one girl, who is fluent in English.
>
> But for a boy who moved here from Puerto Rico a year ago, it's not easy to express in English what he has learned.
>
> "I learned that," he said, pointing to the blackboard.
>
> "What's that?" asked Ms. Trigo.
>
> "Circumference," he said.
>
> "What's the formula for circumference?" she asked.
>
> The youth mumbled an answer.
>
> "What's the number for pi?" she asked.
>
> "Catorce [fourteen]," he said in Spanish.
>
> "Tell me in English. Did you write it down?"
>
> "Three-point-one-four," he said, after checking his notes.
>
> "Excellent."[64]

[64]Zehr (2006), p. 15.

A student who has not yet mastered his numbers in English is still a beginner and needs basic ESL. By Krashen's definition, sheltered instruction is inappropriate for this boy. He would be much better off in a bilingual math class, where he might actually learn something. Trapped in SIOP, he is likely to remain far behind his mainstream classmates.

Who Needs Theory?

OF COURSE, THERE IS NO REASON why the creators of SIOP must adopt either the Comprehension Hypothesis or the original concept of sheltered instruction. They are certainly entitled to challenge Krashen's version and to propose their own. To be credible, however, they must grapple with the theoretical issues of how their model works to advance second language acquisition as well as academic learning. This they fail to do.

Here is where theory matters. It enables consistency in the use of methodologies and strategies. Knowing whether a particular classroom activity succeeds or fails is not enough. In order to replicate it, to refine it, or to replace it, we need to know why. Theory is what provides that explanation (if not, it needs to be rethought). Teaching without a pedagogical rationale becomes a process of trial and error. It is like trying to navigate without a map or instruments; you can never be sure where you are and course corrections become unreliable. Paradoxically, despite SIOP's extreme prescriptiveness, the model fails to offer clear guidance. Its "30 features and eight components" add up to less than a coherent whole.

What would constitute a theoretically driven approach that avoids the pitfalls of SIOP? For one answer, see the ENGAGE Framework outlined in Appendix A *(pp. 59–70)*. What would it look like in practice? Appendix B *(pp. 71–80)* provides a middle school unit that illustrates many possibilities of engaging students in exploring the Amazon Rainforest that the fictional Mr. Montoya failed to exploit.

5 SIOP in Practice: Micromanaging Instruction

S O MUCH FOR OUR THEORETICAL OBJECTIONS TO SIOP. But what about its application in the classroom? Undeniably, some teachers are enthusiastic about the model. Perhaps SIOP, despite its eclecticism, includes tips and techniques that can be beneficial in educating English learners. So it is important to examine, in practice, how SIOP affects the experience of teaching and learning.

This raises the question of how to identify classrooms where the model is being faithfully applied. We could have randomly chosen for analysis a school or district that has adopted SIOP. But how would we determine whether the implementation was typical? SIOP's authors claim that teachers generally need two to three years of training to become "high implementers," capable of using all 30 features in each lesson.[65] Where can such practitioners be found? Fortunately, Echevarría, Vogt, and Short provide numerous sample lesson plans, both in their publications and online.[66] Most helpful is a video produced by the Center for Applied Linguistics.[67] It presents lessons by six actual teachers to illustrate SIOP's features and components, along with commentary by

[65] Echevarría et al. (2013), p. 283.
[66] Center for Applied Linguistics (n.d.c).
[67] *Helping English Learners Succeed* (2002).

the model's developers. These examples are clearly intended to show SIOP at its best. As such, they are quite revealing.

Four of the videotaped lessons are drawn from middle school, one from elementary school, and one from high school. Respectively, they focus on subjects including "World War II and the Atomic Bomb," "The English Settle America," "Magnets," "The Achievements of the Sumerian Empire," "Addition Stories," and "Parts of the Cell." Most, if not all, of these subjects have a potential to interest and engage students at various ages and grade levels. Let's see how SIOP seizes, or misses, those opportunities. We have grouped our analysis around the model's Eight Components.

Lesson Preparation

In CAL's video and sample lessons, each class begins with the SIOP-required posting of daily language and content objectives on the board (Features 1 and 2). The teacher then goes over the objectives in detail, sometimes asking a student to read them aloud or telling the class to record the objectives in their notebooks. Key vocabulary words are highlighted for preteaching. Rather than conceptual understanding, the content objectives usually involve a simplistic regurgitation of facts or the performance of planned routines. Here are some examples from middle and high school: "Students will identify four achievements of the Sumerians ... conduct an experiment according to directions ... describe the characteristics of the Taínos." Language objectives are rudimentary as well: "Students will discuss topics in small groups ... classify people and places ... read nutrition facts on a cereal box ... skim text for information."

Even if these objectives were age- and grade-appropriate, why waste class time by discussing specific, predetermined outcomes for each lesson? What does this accomplish other than to impose strict boundaries on the curriculum? SIOP's authors imply that, without a conscious emphasis on objectives, teachers and students would get lost and forget what they are supposed to be doing. Who knows what might happen if a class strayed from its preplanned path? Spontaneity, discovery, fun? Students could get the wrong idea about school—for example, it's not all about "rigor" and tedium. Or, at least, it doesn't have to be.

Is there anything wrong with consciously setting goals for learning? Of course not. The problems begin when goals are narrowly prescribed and enforced. In a truly creative lesson, teachers may plan and students may participate with separate aims in mind. For example, a Readers Theater performance of "Rappaccini's Daughter," the Hawthorne story, can serve to cultivate an appreciation of literature from another time, stimulate discussion about the ethics of scientific experiments, enable students to showcase their thespian talents, foster English acquisition in a comprehensible context, and create an enjoyable experience—all at the same time.[68] There is no reason why a specific learning objective must limit the possibilities or why teachers and students must be motivated in identical ways. It's only natural for teachers and students to have different objectives. This is why teachers are needed: to use their broader knowledge and vision and worldly experience to engage students intellectually, encouraging them to explore what excites them while also guiding them in productive directions.

No doubt some educators welcome the security that micromanagement provides. "I can't imagine teaching a class now without having those objectives there," says one teacher in CAL's video. "It's my safety net." But what kind of teaching does this inspire? Behaviorist teaching. According to SIOP, language and content objectives should be "observable and measurable." They should be the focus of "explicit instruction ... aligned" to state standards and tests. Posting them on the board should send a clear message to students about "what they are supposed to learn each day."[69] Welcome to the totally controlled, prescribed, joyless classroom.

Building Background

LINKING INSTRUCTION TO STUDENTS' BACKGROUND experiences and prior learning (Features 7 and 8) is a widely practiced technique, hardly unique to SIOP. Good teachers understand that learning—as opposed

---

[68] For an illustration of how Readers Theater can be used effectively with English learners, see Reyes (2013).

[69] Echevarría et al. (2013), pp. 27, 37.

to memorization—is a process of making connections between what we know (or think we know) and the new information that we encounter. It means testing preconceptions against experience and, when appropriate, making adjustments in our worldview.

Yet SIOP seldom makes this *conceptual* use of students' prior learning and experience. Usually, it stresses little more than factual recall, or it merely attempts to fill gaps in children's knowledge before the lesson begins. Most often it involves an emphasis on the explicit teaching of language; preteaching vocabulary is classified as an essential way to "build background" (Feature 9). Take, for example, a 6th grade lesson on European "settlement" of the Americas that appears on CAL's video. The teacher begins by eliciting family stories from her advanced-beginner English learners, asking for "reasons why people come to the U.S." It's a promising start, which seems to engage the class about an authentic issue that interests the students. But their enthusiasm soon wanes as they are asked to write their answers—a big challenge at their level of English proficiency—and to predict which reason will be most "common" (after the word *common* is pretaught). Then "background-building" shifts to classifying words from the textbook as people or places. Finally, students are asked to copy the words into their journals. For homework they are assigned to skim the next chapter—another inappropriate task for beginning English learners—and to match people and places in a graphic organizer.

Here is a subject that should have captivated a middle-school class of immigrant students, a natural way of drawing on (and valuing) their prior knowledge and experience. Because they are beginners, however, they are not ready for a stimulating class taught entirely in English. So instruction is watered down to an early-elementary level and turned into an explicit language lesson that is largely bereft of academic content. Vocabulary is taught abstractly rather than in context, a prescription for boredom and disengagement. This is not sheltered subject matter instruction in any meaningful sense.

Entirely missing from this component—and from SIOP itself—is an emphasis on reading as a major source of vocabulary and background knowledge. Toward the end of the SIOP manual, Echevarría et al. note:

"Research suggests that English learners need systematic, high-quality literacy instruction from the start" (p. 240). Oddly enough, that need is never directly addressed by any of SIOP's 30 Features. Nor is *free voluntary reading* by students even mentioned in SIOP publications, despite research showing its important contribution to second language acquisition.[70] Again it's the skill-building philosophy that dominates.

Comprehensible Input

ADDING TO THE THEORETICAL CONFUSION, SIOP's creators conflate Krashen's concept of comprehensible input with the concept of sheltering. That is, they confuse the *source* of language acquisition—which can take many forms, both inside and outside the classroom—with teaching techniques to facilitate it by making input comprehensible. This seems to be another example of the transmission mentality at work; it assumes that language acquisition has to involve a teacher-centered lesson. In fact, English learners encounter meaningful messages in many contexts apart from formal instruction, such as interactions in the community, exposure to media, and of course, recreational reading. Ignoring these sources of comprehensible input, SIOP focuses instead on explicit instruction, as illustrated in a 7th grade science class highlighted on CAL's video.

The lesson involves magnets and their ability to attract certain metals. As usual in SIOP classrooms, it begins with an extended discussion of language and content objectives, along with a preview of vocabulary. The teacher has written EXTRACT on a large card and posted it across her chest. She pronounces the word several times. In SIOP, "repeated exposure" is considered a key source of comprehensible input. While it's true that encountering new vocabulary in various meaningful contexts can facilitate acquisition, that's not what happens in this classroom. Instead, the teacher asks her students, who are described as intermediate English learners, to guess what "extract" means. The only context provided is limited to the sentence stating the lesson objective: "Today we will use a magnet to extract the iron that is added to the breakfast cereal." The teacher also describes "strategies to take the word apart ... the prefix, suf-

[70]See, e.g., Krashen (2004), pp. 146–149.

fix, and root." But despite the time she devotes to preteaching, none of the students are able to provide a correct answer before the video cuts away.

Next comes a passage read aloud about magnets, accompanied by factual comprehension questions about the text. This is intended to set up the lesson's centerpiece, an experiment to see how much iron can be separated from breakfast cereal using a magnet. Students are given a worksheet with step-by-step instructions, which involve crushing and soaking the cereal, then extracting and weighing the iron filings. Then they are told to graph their findings and record them on the board. Finally, the class is asked to discuss the scientifically pointless question, "What can we conclude about the manufacturers' claims of the amount of iron in each box of cereal?"

The idea here seems to be that "hands-on" activities are another way to make input comprehensible. Such strategies can indeed be effective, especially in a basic ESL class, where physical actions provide important clues to meaning. Bear in mind, however, that sheltered instruction is about teaching language through subject matter—and not just any language, but the specialized vocabulary and syntax needed for success in school. Hands-on activities can help, but only to the extent they support academic learning. In this case, the experiment may be fun for kids, or at least offer a break from teacher-centered instruction. Yet the content is negligible. What is the point, other than to show that breakfast cereal contains metallic particles?[71] The lesson could have been conceptually linked to the nature of magnetism (or nutrition, or cell metabolism, or chemical elements). Why not choose an activity that, for example, visually illustrates a magnetic field using iron filings? Or that demonstrates how magnetism is used to generate electricity, turn an electric motor, or make music speakers possible? Hands-on need not mean dumbed-down. The point of sheltering, after all, is to help English learners acquire academic language. For that, they need grade-appropriate lessons.

SIOP does stress several well-known techniques for making instruction comprehensible: "Use gestures, body language, pictures, and objects

---

[71]The iron particles are added by cereal manufacturers to "fortify" their products so they can advertise that consumers are getting a needed nutrient. In fact, metallic iron is poorly absorbed as compared with the ionic iron that the human body can readily use; O'Shea (2013).

to accompany speech. ... Simplify sentence structures." For beginners, "slow down [the] rate of speech, use pauses, and enunciate clearly." For more advanced English learners, "use a rate of speech that is normal for a regular classroom."[72] Yet the authors fail to explain how such modifications can work simultaneously with learners at varying levels of English—a typical SIOP classroom—other than to recommend that teachers tailor their speech to the proficiency of each individual student. Hardly a practical solution. And—need it be pointed out?—a constant emphasis on simplifying the language of instruction is likely to shortchange native speakers of that language. Are the parents of English-proficient children in SIOP classrooms made aware of this problem?

Strategies

IN THEORY, THERE'S NOTHING OBJECTIONABLE—or original—about SIOP Features 13, 14, and 15: *Ample opportunities provided for students to use learning strategies; Scaffolding techniques consistently used, assisting and supporting student understanding;* and *A variety of questions or tasks that promote higher-order thinking skills.* For example, "cognitive learning strategies," as defined by SIOP, include routine study habits—used by many students regardless of language proficiency—such as note-taking, outlining, highlighting, previewing a text, and using graphic organizers. The problems arise in the mechanistic ways in which the strategies are applied.

A lesson on "The Achievements of the Sumerian Empire," featured on CAL's video, provides an excellent illustration of the misuse—through overuse—of learning strategies. Indeed, the application of tree maps, cue cards, pictures, and sentence strips is so extensive that there is almost no time left to talk about the Sumerians. No background about that civilization is offered, nor any hint about why it might be worthwhile to study, nor any connection to the Mideast of today.[73] Clearly, a focus on the mechanics of learning is distracting students from a focus on meaning. Imagine trying to read a text and being inter-

---

[72]Echevarría et al. (2013), pp. 97–98, 101.

[73]Possibly such matters had been addressed in a previous lesson, but it's not evident from the narration or the class discussion presented in CAL's video.

rupted after every few sentences to answer questions, make predictions, or identify key vocabulary. SIOP encourages such intrusions in practically every one of its sample lesson plans. These so-called "strategies" betray a thorough misunderstanding of sheltering and scaffolding. They are detrimental both for students' language acquisition and for their engagement with academic content.

Since this 6th grade class consists of beginners and advanced beginners in English and, for the most part, they lack the words to explain the Sumerians' achievements, the teacher has prepackaged responses on cards for students to recite, copy, or paste into graphic organizers. Apparently, she believes that giving them a list of possible answers in advance is a form of scaffolding. Despite SIOP's lip service to fostering "higher-order thinking skills," the only departure from rote learning is when the teacher asks her class to venture an opinion about which achievement is most important. How they should be expected to provide a well-thought-out answer is unclear, following a lesson that includes very little of substance about the Sumerians. In any case, their English is too rudimentary—especially in a subject like social studies—to gain much benefit from sheltered instruction. What's more, the teacher is a fast talker whose complicated directions reveal little understanding of techniques to make herself comprehensible.

It's hard to view this lesson as anything other than educational malpractice. So why do SIOP's authors present it as exemplary? No doubt they approve of its tightly scripted format and its explicit and extensive use of so-called learning strategies. Also, like other SIOP lessons, it stresses the mechanics of language at the expense of content, directing students to "practice" their English in four ways: reading, writing, listening, and speaking. Once again, SIOP represents a reversal of the original concept of sheltered instruction, as defined by Krashen: a way of teaching language naturally and indirectly by focusing students' attention on comprehensible and interesting subject matter.

Interaction

IN EFFECT, SIOP ASKS TEACHERS to do the impossible. First, it hands them a 30-item checklist to guide them through each lesson and to ensure that predetermined language and content objectives are met.

Then it cautions that lessons may not be "teacher-dominated"; instead they should provide plenty of time for open-ended participation by students. Classrooms must be tightly scripted and controlled yet also encourage interactive learning.[74] How these contradictory feats can be performed simultaneously is never explained.

CAL's video illustrates how unworkable this approach can be in practice. Introducing a 1st grade math lesson entitled "Addition Stories," the teacher goes over the day's objectives, which include children's mastery of the words *first, then,* and *together.* Not exactly addition words, but ... whatever. Next she recites the following: "One little apple up in a tree. Two more came. Now there are three." She divides students into pairs facing each other. One group is asked to place apples on a flannel board while reciting the "story," a nonsensical rhyme more appropriate for preschool than 1st grade. The other group is told to write the corresponding equations on a white board. Then partners are swapped and the process is repeated—and repeated and repeated—with additional apples and role reversals. Although there is some chatter among the children, several of whom seem bewildered by the convoluted procedures, it hardly rises to the level of "interaction and discussion," much less the "elaborated responses" envisioned by SIOP.

Another lesson, for advanced English learners in 7th and 8th grades, attempts to stimulate discussion about the dropping of atomic bombs on Japan during World War II. Students are given passages to read, then divided into groups and told to conduct debates about whether the ends justified the means. In concept, such a lesson could be both engaging and thought-provoking, while providing lots of comprehensible input in academic English. Unfortunately, in this case, the "interactions" are planned and orchestrated by the SIOP teacher, who has written "adapted texts" with arguments pro and con. Students are essentially asked to choose among (and parrot) prescripted positions rather than encouraged to freely discuss their own ideas. For several, the lack of engagement is obvious. SIOP again reduces English learners to passive receptors of official knowledge.

[74] SIOP Feature 16: *Frequent opportunities for interaction and discussion between teacher/student and among students, which encourage elaborated responses about lesson concepts.*

Practice & Application

IN ANOTHER ATTEMPT TO DEMONSTRATE its break with traditional pedagogies, SIOP requires *Hands-on materials and/or manipulatives provided for students to practice using new content and knowledge* (Feature 20) and *Activities provided for students to apply content and language knowledge* (Feature 21). These techniques sound rather progressive—until we encounter what SIOP's creators consider to be exemplary lessons. When it comes to classroom practice, SIOP remains wedded to the behaviorist paradigm in which student learning must be tightly monitored and controlled. The authors even cite behaviorism guru Madeline Hunter ("a renowned expert in teaching methods"), who warns that "new learning is like wet cement, it can be easily damaged. A mistake at the beginning of learning can have long-lasting consequences that are hard to eradicate."[75] This static conception is contradicted by recent research showing that brain development occurs through the continual proliferation and "pruning" of neural connections.[76] It is also at odds with progressive teaching, which encourages students to inquire and explore freely, to challenge preconceived notions (their own as well as those of others), and to treat mistakes as learning opportunities.

A high-school biology lesson on CAL's video, "Parts of the Cell," is offered as a well-implemented example of hands-on practice and application. Like all SIOP lessons, it begins with a laborious introduction of language and content objectives. "We're going to read them and then we're going to copy them," the teacher tells his class of advanced-beginner and intermediate English learners. The students duly comply. After asking a series of factual questions about the previous lesson, he divides the class into small groups and hands out instructions on creating a physical model of a plant or animal cell. Students are provided a rubric on how they will be graded on tasks such as labeling the cell's parts and functions. Construction materials include cardboard, foam, paper, glue, Play-Doh, fruits, vegetables, and cakes. For guidance, students are encouraged to consult illustrations in their textbook, as well as models constructed by other classes.

[75]Echevarría et al. (2013), pp. 174–175.
[76]Johnson et al. (2009).

The teacher then circulates among the groups praising their creative efforts. Indeed, this lesson is essentially an art project—nothing wrong with that, but there is limited scientific content. In essence, students are taking a textbook diagram and making it three-dimensional. The activity is all about memorizing and identifying features of the cell, about transmitting a closed body of knowledge from teacher to students. There's no experimentation, no inquiry, and no conceptual learning.

Lesson Delivery

OUT OF SIOP'S 30 FEATURES, 29 provide specific instructions for teachers. For example: *Content objectives clearly supported by lesson delivery* (Feature 23) and *Language objectives clearly supported by lesson delivery* (Feature 24). As the authors explain, these criteria require plenty of "explicit instruction" to hammer home whatever it is that the lesson is supposed to be transmitting or—to use their preferred term—"delivering." Indeed, *lesson delivery* is a revealing phrase. It implies that students' role is merely to receive knowledge and skills that have been preselected for them by authorities—that is, "aligned to standards." As if "learning" could be wrapped up in a neat package, ready to be dropped off by UPS.

The one SIOP feature that seems logically out of place, since it is not a teaching technique, involves the teacher's impact in the classroom: *Students engaged approximately 90% to 100% of the period* (Feature 25). Such figures convey an impression of precision and authority. Yet where do they come from and how do they relate to sheltered instruction? Why not 80% to 90%? or 60% to 70%? Will learning suffer unless students are "on task" nearly all of the time? Is this goal even achievable? Would allowing an occasional breather from the pursuit of language and content objectives be detrimental? How do SIOP's authors know? Is there any research supporting Feature 25, any "scientifically validated" finding to point to? Or is SIOP simply espousing a philosophy that teachers must keep children's noses to the grindstone as much as possible? To ask these questions is to answer them.

Obviously, engagement is a crucial factor in learning; even more so for children acquiring English, who get little comprehensible input when they are bored, distracted, and alienated from school. Whether engagement can be precisely measured, however, is another matter. According to SIOP's authors, it means that students are paying attention, following directions, participating in groups, and not misbehaving.[77] But is this sufficient? If a lesson stimulates little interest, focusing sustained attention on subject matter becomes a challenge for students, especially when it's in a new language. How much real learning is taking place if they are mostly tuning out? Children may appear to be absorbing the teacher talk when their minds are actually miles away.

SIOP exacerbates the tendency for disengagement with its overemphasis on language mechanics at the expense of subject matter. This problem is obvious in CAL's video. As SIOP requires, the exemplary lessons incorporate all four components of language—listening, speaking, reading, and writing—along with the preteaching of vocabulary. Rarely is there time left for more than a superficial treatment of academic content. Unless students are called upon, their participation is muted, to say the least. Passivity rather than excitement is the norm. In some cases, children seem to be looking away from the teachers as they lecture. No spitballs are flying, it's true, but you have to wonder what will happen tomorrow when the video cameras are gone.

In fairness, we must acknowledge that the SIOP teachers in this video are doing difficult duty. Shackled by a 30-feature checklist, they have limited freedom to depart from a script or to find creative ways to cut through student boredom. For the most part, they even fail to follow SIOP's recommendations to speak slowly and clearly, simplify their language, use gestures and visual aids, and allow wait time for student responses. Sadly, these harried teachers seem to have forgotten the purpose of sheltered instruction: to make academic subjects comprehensible for children acquiring English.

Review & Assessment

CONSISTENT WITH THE BEHAVIORIST APPROACH, SIOP advises teachers to continually "highlight and review" key vocabulary and factual knowledge as they are being explicitly taught. Meanwhile, formal and informal assessments of how well students are absorbing this information must take place throughout and especially at the conclusion of each

[77]Echevarría et al. (2013), pp. 194–195.

lesson. "Regular feedback"—positive or negative reinforcement—should be provided to individual students about their "output," and the output must be "measurable," a key tenet of behaviorist pedagogy. You have to wonder, after all these tedious requirements have been observed, how much energy remains for meaningful teaching and learning, much less any kind of stimulating activity.

In effect, SIOP creates an artificial separation between instruction and assessment. Experienced teachers have learned how to recognize, without excessive amounts of explicit testing, whether students are understanding and participating in class or whether they are struggling and need extra help. Developing such skills is especially important in sheltering instruction. Effective teachers must make lessons accessible at students' level of English while keeping them immersed in academic content so "compelling" that, as Krashen says, they may even forget which language is being used.[78] By contrast, constant repetition and testing of vocabulary and content knowledge are not only unnecessary; they are counterproductive. SIOP-style "review and assessment" waste valuable time and interrupt the flow of a lesson just when it might be getting interesting. Moreover, as noted, forcing second language output by English learners before they are ready is likely to produce anxiety and self-consciousness, raising the affective filter that blocks comprehensible input.

What do SIOP assessments look like in practice? The Center for Applied Linguistics recommends that teachers should begin with "traditional assessments"—worksheets, essentially—and adapt them for English learners. For example, an "adapted assessment" for 1st grade science tells students to categorize objects in columns labeled "Floating" and "Sinking."[79] Instead of words, it uses clip-art images of a bowling ball, a sailboat, coins, leaves, etc. In place of having students write sentences using these objects, it provides sentence stems such as

The bowling ball _____ in water.
The leaves _____ in water.

But what exactly is being tested here? Knowledge about what floats and what sinks or subject-verb agreement: *float* vs. *floats, sink* vs. *sinks?*

[78]Krashen (2011).
[79]Center for Applied Linguistics (n.d.d).

English learners are likely to be further confused by the columns' use of the -*ing* inflection, which in this context prompts them to create ungrammatical sentences. A test of rote learning abstracted from any meaningful context is bad enough, in our view. This crude adaptation makes it even worse.

'TWIOP'

As noted previously, SIOP's developers have aggressively marketed their model to educators in a variety of fields, including foreign language teaching, adult ESL, and two-way bilingual immersion. One might ask: What is the pedagogical rationale? Are there theoretical reasons why this model would work in such diverse classrooms? Or is SIOP like an oldtime patent medicine, good for whatever ails you?

We foresee a few problems with SIOP expansion into new realms. Foreign language and adult ESL educators, for example, should not be expected to teach academic subject matter for which they are normally unprepared. Nor should students in these fields be subjected to such lessons.

Two-way immersion (TWI), a bilingual approach designed to cultivate bilingualism, has little in common with all-English pedagogies designed to assimilate immigrant children. Why combine it with SIOP, which provides no support for student bilingualism? The Center for Applied Linguistics responds that, as "a leader" in both fields, it "has had an interest in merging its expertise in these two areas and in particular, in exploring the SIOP as an effective instructional approach for TWI programs."[80] No theory is offered, only a plan to adapt TWI for SIOP and see what happens. To that end, in 2005, CAL sponsored a project funded by the Goldman Sachs Foundation that involved SIOP trainers, four two-way immersion teachers, and a few of its own researchers to develop a "modified model" called TWIOP. Out of this project came a handbook and sample lesson plans, but still no explanation of why SIOP would be beneficial—or even compatible—in a dual language program.

Like French immersion in Canada, dual immersion—a.k.a. two-way bilingual education—has been quite successful in the United States. Once again, it's important to understand why. Analyzing the reasons for

[80]Howard et al. (2006), p. 1.

a program model's effectiveness is essential before tinkering with adaptations; otherwise its strongest elements could be sacrificed.

As discussed in Chapter 1, the one-way approach used in French immersion makes instruction comprehensible primarily through teacher input in the second language, which is sheltered for students who are at roughly the same level of proficiency. Over time, these Canadian Anglophones achieve basic competence in French,[81] along with grade-level academic performance. By contrast, a two-way bilingual model provides multiple sources of comprehensible input by including both native speakers and learners of each language. Children are enrolled early—ideally in preschool, rarely later than 1st grade. By the time they encounter challenging academic material, they are bilingual to varying degrees and, most likely, intermediate learners of the second language. They also have opportunities for cognitive and academic development in the first language, which do not exist in SIOP or other ESL classrooms.

Another advantage is the key role of collaborative learning; in effective two-way models, students assist each other with language while engaging in joint exploration and discovery. In the process, they come to appreciate different cultures and different ways of approaching problems. Naturally and without explicit coaching, student interaction becomes a form of sheltered instruction. As a result, teachers don't feel pressure to "dumb down" academic content for fear of leaving some children behind. Moreover, since all two-way students are second language learners, power and status differences can be minimized by vigilant educators, creating a level playing field that fosters community. This is not the case in a mixed, all-English classroom, where minority children are inevitably treated as a problem to be solved (or avoided), rather than as a resource for other students.

SIOP offers none of the features that give two-way programs an edge in promoting both language acquisition and academic learning. What would TWIOP offer? In a word: micromanagement. Seeking to duplicate—indeed, expand—SIOP's requirements in both languages, TWIOP proposes "modifications" of three basic types:

---

[81] Studies have shown, however, that students seldom reach native-like levels of French because they usually lack peer models of the language; Cummins (2001 [1979]).

• *"Coordinating instruction in the two program languages to facilitate transfer of skills and ... thematic instruction or careful articulation within units that are taught jointly through both program languages."* Of course, collaboration between teachers of each language is an integral feature of two-way immersion. So is thematic instruction. Nothing new here. What TWIOP would introduce is tight control over both. Rather than allowing the transfer of skills to occur naturally between languages, as it does in well-designed bilingual programs, TWIOP stresses the explicit teaching of skills. "Careful articulation" means that thematic units must be prescripted in every respect. In other words, TWIOP enforces a strict transmission model, just like SIOP.

• *"Articulate clear cultural objectives for each unit."* A focus on cultural knowledge has long been emphasized in two-way bilingual education. But formal study is hardly the only way students expand their multicultural understanding. Some of their most important "lessons" come from the experience of interacting and working with peers from other ethnic groups. By introducing cultural objectives, TWIOP assumes that, in order to learn, children must be indoctrinated in a body of received wisdom.[82]

• *"Explicitly teach some of the TWIOP features so that students can incorporate them while working together in cooperative groups."* What this means is a requirement to train children in using teacher-devised strategies when working with classmates. (TWIOP calls this "peer scaffolding.") Thus, rather than encourage spontaneous, open-ended collaboration among students as they tackle joint projects, TWIOP would prescribe how they must work together. Peer teaching can also create an unhealthy power dynamic among classmates, negating one of the major benefits of two-way programs, in which all students have something to learn from each other.

What does TWIOP look like in practice? Its sample lessons, not sur-

---

[82] Among various pitfalls, the potential for stereotyping stands out. A sample SIOP lesson plan, "Taínos," asks students the culturally myopic question: "What are the characteristics of Americans?" Center for Applied Linguistics (n.d.e).

prisingly, look very much like SIOP sample lessons. Take, for example, a 4th grade social studies class on "The Discourse of Reconstruction: Discrimination, Segregation, and Integration." The subject matter itself has plenty of potential to engage students by presenting a historical topic with present-day relevance. You might reasonably assume that this class would delve right in to post–Civil War events and race relations in ways that would relate to student backgrounds, experiences, and interests. You would be wrong. Remember, this is a SIOP lesson. It must feature explicit instruction in key vocabulary and learning strategies before introducing anything of substance.

Day One of the lesson begins with the following exercise:

> Ask the students to close their eyes and picture a "zorple" in their mind [sic]. Write the word *zorple* on the board, and discuss the fact that this is a nonsense word and therefore they could not know what it means.

Students are directed to read a passage about bike repair using *zorple* and try to figure out what it means from the context. An extended discussion ensues, with the goal of explaining that new words can be decoded from context. Students are then given passages containing the words *discrimination, segregation,* and *integration* and asked to figure out their meanings. Next they enter the definitions on a "vocabulary map," a kind of graphic organizer. Finally, the words are reviewed at length, with students told to indicate their understanding of each definition with a thumbs-up or a thumbs-down. The class ends. Reconstruction has yet to come up.

Day Two begins with a "sorting activity" illustrating causes and effects. A random subject may be used (e.g., the weather is suggested). Children are called to the board to sort sentence strips into columns labeled "Causes" and "Effects," an exercise that assumes 4th graders are unfamiliar with this concept. (SIOPers seem to believe that nothing is ever learned without being explicitly taught.) A vocabulary review follows, going back over the three words introduced on Day One. Students are divided into small groups and asked to discuss: "What cause-and-effect connections can be made between discrimination and segregation?" Each group is then assigned to create and perform a skit illustrating this and other cause-and-effect relationships. Finally, students must write down the definition of each word and use it in a sentence. Again the class ends without any discussion of Reconstruction. No Day Three is outlined, only a promise of "coming lessons" in which students will apply the skills they have learned.

So what can we conclude about this example of TWIOP in practice? First of all, it would be inaccurate to call this a social studies lesson. Nor is it sheltered subject matter instruction, because there's really no subject matter presented. It consists entirely of skill-building exercises disconnected from any real-world content, or anything else likely to interest 4th graders. Intellectually, the lesson is far less challenging than what students would receive in most two-way bilingual classrooms, where grade-level material is normally presented.[83] It's no exaggeration to say that TWIOP, like SIOP, is obsessed with the direct teaching of language at the expense of academic content.

Our verdict: Incorporating the SIOP Model into a viable two-way immersion program would be worse than inappropriate; it would be positively harmful.

[83]For an example of a highly acclaimed two-way program, see Reyes & Crawford (2012).

6 Conclusions

THERE IS NO DOUBT THAT THE SIOP® MODEL has become a highly profitable enterprise. There are serious questions, however, whether that could have happened in a different political environment. SIOP owes much of its success to three factors that have exerted a powerful influence on K–12 education in the United States:

- *Ruthless attacks on bilingual education have prompted many school districts to prefer all-English programs for teaching English learners.* Emerging at the apex of the English Only movement, when voters in three states were passing measures to ban native language instruction, SIOP's timing was auspicious. Although it permits the use of students' native language "to clarify key concepts," this weak form of bilingual instruction has no support in educational research. For the most part, SIOP has been adopted as an alternative to more effective, *bilingual* models—those that can legitimately claim to be "scientifically validated."[84]

- *Today's corporate-driven "reform" movement has made top-down standards and high-stakes testing the drivers of U.S. education policy.* Pearson Education has been among the leading beneficiaries

[84]See, e.g., Rolstad et al. (2005); McField & McField (2014).

of this movement, for example, winning testing contracts worth hundreds of millions of dollars.[85] So has the Center for Applied Linguistics, whose revenues from government grants and "program services"—including SIOP training, consulting, and publications—have nearly tripled since passage of the No Child Left Behind (NCLB) Act of 2001.[86]

• *The teaching profession has come under unprecedented attack by "reformers," bearing much of the blame for so-called "achievement gaps" between low-scoring groups, including English learners, and other students.* The basic message is that, when it comes to making decisions about instruction, teachers' professional judgment is not to be trusted. Ergo, classroom activity needs to be tightly controlled and monitored through rigid procedures, explicit objectives, and daily assessments. Pearson's chief education adviser, Sir Michael Barber, summed up this view in a recent article: "Without ... a systematic, data-driven approach to instruction, teaching remains an imprecise and somewhat idiosyncratic process that is too dependent on the personal intuition and competence of individual teachers."[87]

Under NCLB, all states were required to set detailed academic standards and to mandate annual assessments aligned to those standards. Schools and school districts suddenly faced penalties unless they could demonstrate "adequate yearly progress"—not only for students overall but also for underperforming subgroups, including English language learners. All students were expected to reach higher levels in language arts and math each year until they achieved full "proficiency" by 2014, as measured by tests given almost entirely in English.

[85]Pearson's deal with the Texas Education Agency alone is worth $462 million; Quinton & McGee (2013).

[86]In 2000, CAL's income from these sources totaled $5,878,911. By 2010, it had increased to $16,595,429; Center for Applied Linguistics, Forms 990, FY 2000 and FY2010, downloaded from http://www.eri-nonprofit-salaries.com/index. As a matter of policy, CAL does not publicly itemize its SIOP-related revenue (Terrence Wiley, personal communication).

[87]Hill & Barber (2014), p. 38. The overall theme of this monograph is to describe Pearson's place in what it calls the "new world order" created by digital technologies, globalization, and the hegemonic role of assessment in education.

It is now widely agreed that this system was poorly thought-out and patently unfair. Needless to say, the goal of "all children on grade level" remains very far from being achieved. From the outset, a handful of educators and advocates were pointing out the special distortions created by "holding schools accountable" for the performance of students who were—by definition—less than proficient in English. Yet their complaints have been largely ignored. As a consequence, the law has stigmatized schools that teach large numbers of these children, while encouraging educators to adopt an impoverished curriculum designed primarily to pump up test scores. NCLB has also been a boon for marketers of "teacher-proof" curricula that stress direct instruction, such as skill-building approaches to second language acquisition. It has utterly failed, however, to boost the achievement of English learners relative to that of English-proficient students.[88] Among the most important results of standards-and-test-based accountability, even in states where bilingual education faced no organized opposition, has been to exert strong pressure to adopt all-English approaches. This pressure continues.

SIOP is designed to facilitate, rather than challenge, compliance with current policies. Its detailed language and content objectives, combined with an emphasis on explicit instruction, appeal to school officials whose prime concern is prepping students to score well on state standards tests and, starting in 2014–2015, to tests "aligned" with the Common Core. Other educational goals, such as bilingualism and biliteracy, must take a back seat. Creative teachers need not apply. Student inquiry and discovery receive no support. And, in all likelihood, many children will tune out, learn to hate school, and continue to be left behind.

While SIOP is hardly the only—or even the worst—prepackaged "learning system" on the market for English learners, it has benefited from a level of professional credibility that is, in our view, undeserved. We hope this critique will provide a needed antidote.

[88] According to the National Assessment of Educational Progress, between 2003 and 2013 these gaps actually widened in both reading and math for 4th and 8th grade English learners; for 12th grade English learners they widened between 2005 and 2013; http://nces.ed.gov/nationsreportcard/naepdata.

To summarize our objections, we believe that SIOP:

- Does not provide sheltered instruction in any meaningful sense;
- Has not been "scientifically validated" by solid research;
- Lacks rigorous studies showing that it benefits English language learners;
- Is theoretically contradictory and incoherent as a pedagogical approach;
- Imposes a straitjacket on teachers, limiting their ability to engage students;
- Values a mechanical checklist over professional judgment and experience;
- Encourages a transmission model based in behaviorism;
- Fosters passive rather than active learning;
- Stresses the mechanics of language while watering down academic content;
- Represents a poor substitute for bilingual education; and
- Should be seen as an over-hyped commercial product—not as a promising pedagogy for students.

Appendix A

The ENGAGE Framework for Sheltering and Scaffolding Language the Natural Way

By Sharon Adelman Reyes[89]

THERE ARE MANY EXPLICIT "MODELS" for teaching English language learners. Some can be helpful, especially for novice teachers. A major limitation, however, is that they seldom offer a clear rationale for why a methodology or strategy works, when it can be adapted to student needs or community contexts, or how teachers can create successful approaches of their own.

The ENGAGE Framework takes a different approach. Its aim is not to provide step-by-step recipes for instruction. Rather, it is designed to help teachers develop imaginative ways to engage students in academics while they are acquiring English. At the same time, it is grounded in well-researched theories about language and learning, a starting point for instruction that is both creative and effective. Teachers need to understand not only *what* they are doing but *why* they are doing it.

Consciously or not, all educational methodologies flow from and apply a philosophical approach about teaching and learning. In the ENGAGE Framework, that approach is constructivism and the methodologies are sheltering and scaffolding. Sheltering and scaffolding include

---

[89]Adapted from Reyes (2013) and Reyes & Crawford (2012).

simple techniques—common, everyday practices that become second nature to experienced language teachers. Or they can take the more complex form of strategies, which aim toward a specific pedagogical goal and thus require additional reflection, planning, and organization.

A highly structured, prescriptive model of sheltering and scaffolding is not necessary for effectively educating English learners. In fact, mandating any approach that allows for little deviation is likely to be counterproductive. Just as explicit instruction encourages passive learning, tightly scripted lessons encourage passive teaching. The ENGAGE Framework, by contrast, not only allows for but depends on creativity. It advises teachers on how to adapt and invent new strategies to meet the needs of their students.

Bear in mind that no educational framework or model can encompass every aspect of teaching and learning. Those that claim to do so should be viewed with skepticism. In my experience, the best classrooms are too alive, too vibrant, to be restricted by a single overarching structure. Spontaneity should be welcomed, not squelched in the name of preconceived "objectives," rigid lesson plans, or "research-based" models. I believe that the role of frameworks is simply to provide a conceptual basis for instruction—a purposeful way of using methodologies, strategies, and techniques.

This was my aim in developing the ENGAGE Framework: to create a theoretically grounded approach to sheltering and scaffolding for second language learners. In no way does it exclude the use of other methodologies. In fact, it implies a role for culturally responsive pedagogy and native language instruction, even though they are not key components. The ENGAGE Framework is also compatible with discovery learning, problem-based learning, and other forms of constructivism.

What Is Constructivism?

CONSTRUCTIVISM IS, IN THE WORDS OF mathematics educator Catherine Twomey Fosnot, "a theory about learning, not a description of teaching."[90] Thus there are no specific criteria for program design or ped-

---

[90]Fosnot (2005), p. 33.

agogical practice. Nevertheless, there are several guiding principles with implications in the classroom:

- *Goals.* Constructivism defines learning as the development of deep understanding and the ability to think in critical and creative ways. For educators, this means a primary emphasis on concepts—enabling students to construct meaning through reflection and abstraction—rather than teaching "critical thinking" as a preconceived hierarchy of skills or "cultural literacy" through the memorization of officially sanctioned facts.
- *Cognitive development.* True learning is literally a rewiring of the mind, which can only occur through the active engagement of learners in making sense of their experience. Thus, in constructivist classrooms, students not only answer questions and solve problems by testing hypotheses through investigation, experiment, and collaboration with others. They also generate their own questions, problems, and hypotheses through open-ended exploration.
- *Disequilibrium.* Learning interacts with prior knowledge. It occurs when preconceptions are challenged, when mental models are thrown out of equilibrium by unexpected outcomes. This, in turn, inspires learners to restructure their conceptual framework to resolve the contradictions.
- *Inquiry.* Teachers facilitate the learning process by providing an environment that fosters inquiry and discovery and by supplying the cognitive tools that students may need in their investigations. The latter include "habits of mind" like those encouraged at New York's Central Park East schools, as described by Deborah Meier:

> the question of evidence, or "How do we know what we know?"; the question of viewpoint in all its multiplicity, or "Who's speaking?"; the search for connections and pattern, or "What causes what?"; supposition, or "How might things have been different?"; and, finally, why any of it matters, or "Who cares?"[91]

[91]Meier (1995), p. 50.

• *Social interaction.* While learning is a process of meaning-making in the individual mind, it inevitably occurs in a cultural—or multicultural—context. That is, it builds upon one or more foundations of socially constructed meaning, which often prove to be contradictory. Collaborative learning, especially when it involves children from different languages and cultures, thus provides a stimulating blend of perspectives that can lead to greater understanding.

• *Motivation.* Self-directed learning means exploring what interests the learner—not in a haphazard, chaotic way, but in a purposefully planned community that blurs the line between instructor and instructed. In such classrooms, where everyone participates in the process of discovery, external motivators are rarely necessary. Neither is "behavior management." When stimulated, the internal motivators to learn are far more powerful than the carrots and sticks that drive the transmission model.

Sheltering

SHELTERING IS A METHODOLOGY THAT IS SPECIFIC to the teaching of second language learners. Its goal is to make input comprehensible by communicating messages—ideally, just beyond students' current level of understanding. Linguists hypothesize that there is a "natural order" of language acquisition. Generally speaking, complex grammatical forms become comprehensible later, and thus are acquired later, than simpler forms. Providing English learners large amounts of comprehensible input enables them to progress to what Stephen Krashen calls *i + 1,* the next step in the natural order of language acquisition.[92]

How is this accomplished in the classroom?

• *Focus on content; don't focus on form.* Students receive more comprehensible input when their attention is focused on meaningful activities and relevant information, rather than on repetitive drills, flash cards, and similar exercises. Explicit instruction in grammar and vocabulary may produce apparent gains, at least in the short term—for example, an ability to recall linguistic rules

[92]Krashen (1985).

when given time to do so—but it is not sufficient to equip students to use a second language in real-life communicative situations.

• *Don't worry if students make errors in grammar, vocabulary, or pronunciation.* Making mistakes is a natural part of learning. If sufficiently exposed to comprehensible input, students will acquire correct forms on their own. Besides being ineffective, error correction has undesirable side effects. By making students anxious and self-conscious, it raises the "affective filter" that blocks comprehensible input.

• *Don't worry about output.* Second language students should not be forced to talk. In fact, a "silent period" of up to six months is normal for beginners. Speech production will occur naturally when they are ready to show off their competence. It results from, rather than causes, language acquisition.

• *Shelter through language use.* Techniques include pacing, pausing, gesturing, facial expression, tone, rephrasing, and redundancy. Avoid needless complexity in sentence structure. Do frequent comprehension checks.

• *Shelter through context, hands-on experiences, and visuals.* Introduce new vocabulary by using it in familiar situations. Enhance context through manipulatives, realia, games, field trips, and peer support. Make ample use of photos, drawings, charts, calendars, graphic organizers, and appropriate technology.

Scaffolding

SCAFFOLDING IS A METHODOLOGY THAT IS APPLICABLE to the teaching of all students, including second language learners. In a constructivist framework, it functions to make the curriculum comprehensible while encouraging students to explore, invent, and discover—in short, to help them make meaning from experience. This process requires a knowledgeable adult to support children or adolescents through each new phase of learning. The constructivist teacher keeps activities within the zone of proximal development, providing and removing support as appropriate, while incorporating as much student choice as possible.

How are these principles of scaffolding applied in practice?

• *Build on what students already know or believe.* An important principle of constructivism is that knowledge is never acquired in a vacuum. We take in, evaluate, and organize new information in relation to the ideas we already possess. Often this process results in conflicts, which in turn become the source of different or deeper insights. To help students take full advantage of such learning opportunities, teachers can assist them in clarifying what they currently know or believe as the foundation for new knowledge.

• *Stress conceptual understanding.* True learning involves cognitive change. It means building and rebuilding mental structures as we interpret the world around us. Thus constructivist teachers recognize the importance of elevating projects and discussions to a conceptual level, encouraging students to reflect and generalize about their experience.

• *Provide expert modeling.* By thinking out loud, model your own processes of critical questioning, problem-posing, and conceptual analysis. Demonstrate how to perform tasks and coach students who are grappling with especially difficult ones. Bring outside professionals into the classroom to describe projects, experiments, and other learning activities.

• *Encourage questioning.* Take a skeptical approach toward official knowledge and "expert" opinion, modeling the habits of critical analysis. Ask open-ended questions that lead to new and unexpected lines of inquiry and let students pursue their own answers. Encourage them to pose their own problems. When the opportunity arises, turn those problems into research projects.

• *Give feedback at appropriate times.* After providing children ample opportunities to solve problems on their own, step in before they become frustrated and lose motivation. Offer advice that will help them advance their understanding. When students continue to struggle, coach them on ways to overcome conceptual or linguistic barriers.

• *Create opportunities for all students to participate.* Teachers must work hard to ensure that no student is excluded from an activity because of language difficulties and, at the same time, that no student is bored by oversimplified content. Several techniques have proved effective: Give students plenty of options. Make learning a collective enterprise by including problems that can be solved with peer support. Encourage students who have become expert in a subject or skill to assist their classmates.

• *Turn mistakes into opportunities.* Make it clear that mistakes are normal, everyday occurrences—and not just for students, but for teachers as well. When analyzed and discussed, mistakes can also provide an important stimulus for learning because they prompt us to rethink our existing ideas.

Classroom Environment

NO METHODOLOGY, HOWEVER EFFECTIVE, can work wonders on its own. Teaching and learning are among the most complex of human activities, in part because they occur in a multiplicity of contexts that often matter as much as instruction itself. To make sheltering and scaffolding as effective as possible, here are some guidelines for shaping the classroom environment:

• *Lower the affective filter.* An environment that feels safe and secure is essential to authentic learning. Arts-based activities, in which there are many "correct" answers, can play an important role here. But any lesson that is compelling and engaging can lower the affective filter by making students forget they are learning in a second language.

• *Incorporate lots of free voluntary reading.* Krashen notes that reading is the most effective way to acquire academic language. Studies have also shown that when books are freely chosen by students, their reading tends to be more extensive.

• *Ensure that resources are available.* Besides being equipped with movable furniture and ample space for learners to interact, classrooms should be well-supplied with books on subjects of interest to students; maps, charts, and other visuals; computers, software, Internet connections, and multimedia; materials that stimulate artistic activities; and items from the natural world, such as fish tanks, terrariums, and ant colonies. Other key resources include trips to museums, zoos, aquariums, plays, concerts, science fairs, and various community- and family-oriented events.

• *Use authentic assessment.* Incorporate informal, ongoing assessments to gauge students' day-to-day progress in a low-stress environment. Focus primarily on their responses and performance in classroom activities rather than on off-the-shelf commercial tests.

The graphic on the facing page shows the basic elements of the ENGAGE Framework, beginning with a large star representing the constructivist philosophy that guides it. The nearby hexagons depict four important features of the classroom environment. At the bottom of the graphic are ovals that identify sheltering and scaffolding techniques used informally throughout the day. These are incorporated into the strategies at the center of the diagram, a progression of which leads toward a specific curricular goal.

Finally, it's important to reiterate that the ENGAGE Framework can be applied to virtually any type of academic content. My hope is that educators will use it as a guide to teaching language not only through the creative arts, but across the curriculum in language arts, math, science, and social studies.

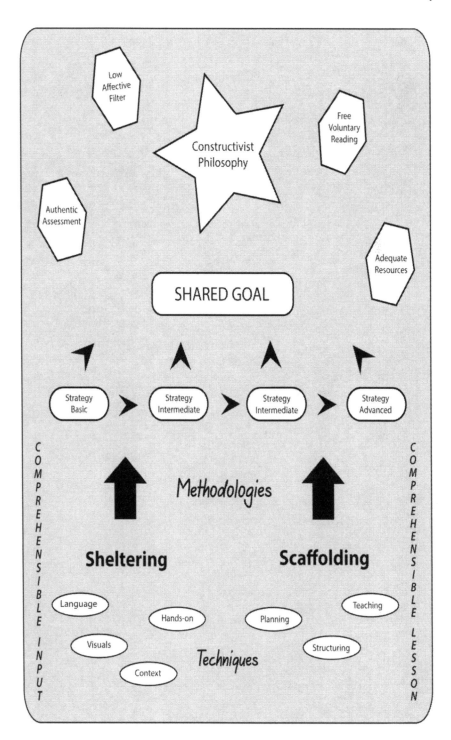

Sheltering Overview

Goal	To make second language input comprehensible to the learner	
Guidelines	Focus on content; don't focus on form Don't worry if students make mistakes Don't worry about output	
Techniques	*With language*	Pacing and pauses Clarity of speech Tone and inflection Facial expression Gesture and body language Dramatic expression Introducing vocabulary in context Simple grammatical structure Tense control Redundancy and rephrasing Sentence expansion Idea expansion Sequence Comprehension checks
	With context	Peer support Field trips and excursions Games and activities Technology
	With visuals	Photographs Pictures Graphs Charts Tables Maps Timelines Diagrams Graphic organizers
	With hands-on	Realia Objects Manipulatives

Scaffolding Overview

Goals To make curriculum comprehensible to the learner

To encourage self-directed learning by providing assistance to students, enabling them to think independently, critically, and creatively

Guidelines Keep activities within the zone of proximal development

Provide and remove support as appropriate

Incorporate as much choice as possible

Techniques *Planning* Begin with simple tasks to boost students' confidence

Plan a logical sequence of activities

Foster active rather than passive learning

Focus on process, not product

Structuring Include problems that can be solved with peer support

Enable all students to participate at their own linguistic and academic level

Incorporate response activities

Teaching Build on prior knowledge

Stress conceptual understanding

Model your own thought process by "thinking out loud"

Demonstrate how to perform tasks

Use expert models

Pose problems, invite questions

Provide feedback, offer explanations

Coach learners who continue to struggle

Transform student mistakes into learning opportunities

Sheltering and Scaffolding Strategies

Creative Arts
Choral Reading
Jazz Chants
Pantomime
Puppetry
Readers Theater
Structured Poetry

Language Arts
Dialogue Journals
Jigsaw
KWL
Literature Circles
Read Alouds
Response Journals
Think Alouds
Think-Pair-Share
T-Journals

Social Studies
Fishbowl
Jigsaw
KWL
Mock Trials
Oral Histories
Response Journals
Think-Pair-Share
Timelines

Mathematics
Board Games
Learning Centers
Response Journals
Student Generated Word Problems
Think Aloud
Think-Pair-Share

Science
Experiments
Jigsaw
KWL
Learning Centers
Observation Journals
Think-Pair-Share

Appendix B

Discovering the Amazon

A Middle-School Unit
Applying the ENGAGE Framework
By Sharon Adelman Reyes

R OSA VALIENTE BEGAN THE ACADEMIC YEAR with excitement. As a science and social studies teacher, she was now assigned to a 7th grade classroom of intermediate English learners, and the curriculum included a unit on the Amazon Rainforest. Just last year she had followed the news on sightings of an uncontacted group of indigenous peoples on the border between Peru and Brazil. This provoked her interest in Ann Patchett's novel *State of Wonder*, set in that same rainforest. Over the summer she had been spellbound by the book. It inspired her to compile a reading list for herself consisting of various kinds of literature set in the Amazon *(see sidebar, next page)*.

Now was the perfect opportunity to explore her developing interest in the region and to take others along for the figurative journey. Because she would be teaching a sheltered class for English learners, Ms. Valiente knew she would have to carefully design the curriculum so that, rather than struggling with the language, her students would become captivated and perhaps even enchanted by the subject matter.

Although there were state-mandated science and social studies standards for 7th grade, they could all be subsumed under her own goals for the class: to interest the students in the natural and human geography of the Amazon Rainforest, to facilitate an understanding of how that region is connected to their own lives, and to provide an opportunity for them to express opinions on the topic to a wider audience, if they so desired. The unit she had in mind would involve students in planning their own projects, all leading toward the unit goals. Many of their inquiries would naturally "cover" the state standards in science and social studies. But Ms. Valiente also decided to keep a running log, so she could find opportunities to weave in those that were overlooked.

Although the school science textbook had a chapter on the Amazon Rainforest, it was not designed with English learners in mind. In any case, Ms. Valiente thought that using a textbook as the main source on such an exciting topic would limit possibilities for her students and diminish their interest. She suspected that many more stimulating resources were available for teaching about the Amazon Rainforest. A quick Internet search turned up sites such as PBS.org that offered a wealth of such materials.

To introduce the unit, however, Ms. Valiente wanted an activity that was not text-based and that would have strong emotional appeal. She decided to use a variation of the Visual Journey strategy[93] to shelter language by using background sounds of the natural and human environment. She checked the Smithsonian's "Folkways" collection online and discovered a CD entitled *The Dry Season: Toucan and Jay—Sounds of a Tropical Rainforest*. From

Literature Set in the Amazon

Novels

At Play in the Fields of the Lord
Peter Mathiessen
Love in the Time of Cholera
Gabriel García Marquez
Macunaíma
Mario de Andrade
The Sea and the Jungle
Henry Tomlinson
Maíra
Darcy Ribeiro

Film

At Play in the Fields of the Lord

Opera

Florencia in the Amazon (based on *Love in the Time of Cholera*)
Houston Grand Opera

[93]Reyes (2013).

the website of Arte Amazonia,[94] she chose percussive instruments and an authentic recording of music from a tribe living deep within the Amazon. She also located an extensive collection of color photographs taken in the Amazon Rainforest.[95] Finally, she researched the region's natural elements and peoples so she could blend in her own commentary while the recordings played in the background.

Now she was ready to begin.

••••••••••

Ms. Valiente pulls down the shades and dims the classroom lights, telling her students that they are going on a journey in their imaginations. "Close your eyes, relax, and listen," she says. Then she plays sounds from the Amazon Rainforest. Using a soft voice, she tells them to note the specific sounds they hear, think about the quality of the air, and imagine the colors that surround them. "Where do you think you are?" she asks. "Don't tell me now; we'll save it for later."

Fading out the first recording, Ms. Valiente slowly turns up the volume on another. This is a recording of indigenous peoples of the Amazon Rainforest chanting and using authentic percussive instruments. Again she verbally guides the students into thinking about the sounds they are hearing. After slowly turning down the volume until all is silent in the room, she brings up the lights.

Ms. Valiente invites the students to share where they have imagined themselves to be. There are a few tentative responses—"Florida ... South America ... Africa"— but nobody knows for sure. Their teacher still isn't telling; instead she brings out more clues. First are indigenous instruments, such as a cacho *(seed pod rattle) and* maracas *(made from calabash and filled with achira seeds). Then come photos of insects, animals, plants, and geographic features. "The Amazon!" shouts one student. Ms. Valiente smiles and arranges the students in groups, distributing the items for them to examine and pass around, circulating among them and helping to guide their discussions.*

[94]http://www.arte-amazonia.com/music; also a source for indigenous crafts, videos, books, and more.

[95]Available at http://kids.mongabay.com.

THE TEACHER HAS SHELTERED new vocabulary with sound, visuals, and authentic objects. Listening to the groups conversing was part of her plan to assess her students' prior knowledge and link it to their background experiences. She expected to encounter stereotypes of indigenous people and of the Amazon region. But she also knew that a number of the children had an indigenous heritage, and she was curious to see how much they knew about it. Further, she hoped that the parents of some of her South American students would have relevant knowledge that they would want to share with the class.

••••••••

After the small groups have had a chance to handle and discuss all of the items, Ms. Valiente finally confirms that they represent the Amazon Rainforest. She points out this region on the classroom globe and on maps she has found at the Raintree website.[96] Again she displays the images and this time gives a little information about each one. Then she holds up the percussive instruments, using a series of questions as a basis for conversation:

- *Who do you think uses these?*
- *What do you think they are made from?*
- *What do you think they are used for?*
- *Where do you think these people live?*
- *What language do you think they speak?*
- *Do you think they have ever encountered people from outside the rainforest?*
- *Do you think their lives have changed in the past 20 years? 10 years? 5 years?*

••••••••

Ms. VALIENTE HAS USED CONTEXT to shelter her speech, as well as linguistic techniques such as pacing, avoiding complex grammatical structures, and using dramatic expression.[97] Meanwhile, she has scaffolded

[96] http://www.rain-tree.com/schoolreports.htm.

[97] See summary chart on sheltering, p. 68.

her instruction, moving from sound to visuals and realia and then to discussion. As the lesson progresses, she hopes to continue scaffolding to the point that students are motivated and able to initiate, complete, and present a research project.[98]

••••••••••

By now Ms. Valiente is beginning to see preferences in regard to topics. She groups students accordingly at student desks pushed together to function as tables. Each group receives a large piece of paper and a marker, appoints a scribe, and brainstorms questions on its topic. Ms. Valiente circulates among the groups to assist. She pays no attention at this point to grammatical or linguistic mistakes. Her focus is on helping each group formulate good content questions and decide which is the most intriguing. With her guidance, each group rewrites its chosen question as a focus for research. She avoids using the term objective, *which implies a preselected body of knowledge. Instead, she prefers the scientific term* research question, *which conveys the message: "finding things out that we would like to know."*

The teacher distributes more chart paper. This shifts the classroom focus naturally from content to language, as students express the desire to write their objectives in a grammatically correct manner. They rely on the monitor function for writing and editing, with assistance from their teacher. Ms. Valiente does no direct instruction in grammar, but she freely answers students' direct questions about "correct" English.

Each group appoints a scribe to print its research question (or group of related questions) neatly for classroom display. For example, one group posts the following: "Are there tribes in the Amazon Rainforest that nobody knows?" After some discussion facilitated by Ms. Valiente, they decide on a sequence of research questions: "Are there tribes in the Amazon Rainforest who have not had contact with the outside world? Are there tribes who have had contact with the outside world only recently? If so, what happened when the tribes made contact with the outside world?"

[98]See summary chart on scaffolding, p. 69.

Ms. Valiente continues to circulate among the groups. She scaffolds the development of research questions by modeling her own thought process on each topic, challenging students to push them further in their own thinking, and answering a variety of questions, both factual and conceptual. Another group finalizes its research questions as follows: "Why are there so many plant and animal species in the Amazon region? Why are so many of them threatened with extinction? Why is this important to people in the United States?"

Of the three remaining groups, one focuses on natural forces that shaped the geography and geology of the Amazon Basin. Another decides to investigate the relationship between climate and disease along the Amazon River. The last group formulates questions about threats to the rainforest: why they are happening and what is being done about them.

Each group tapes its research questions to a wall in the classroom, then shares its interests with the others. Ms. Valiente leads the class in a discussion of how the groups will investigate their topics. She provides samples of Internet sites (see sidebar, next page) *that are easily accessible for Amazon-related resources, including articles, maps, photographs, and interviews with experts, covering such topics as biodiversity, climate change, and cultural preservation.*

Ms. Valiente emphasizes that these links should be seen as just a starting point or a means of generating further ideas. The students will also need to incorporate information and materials that they discover on their own. She provides a list of possible sources, noting that it is far from exhaustive:

- *Interviews with knowledgeable adults, such as parents, relatives, and friends*
- *Consulates of countries with a geographic presence in the Amazon*
- *Validated Internet research*
- *Internet videos clips, educational DVDs and TV shows, and films that take place in the Amazon*
- *Soundtracks*

Amazon-Related Websites
For Teachers and Students

kids.mongabay.com
Ecology-oriented rainforest lessons for grades 3–5

www.uncontactedtribes.org/evidence
Never-before-seen videos of uncontacted Indians

www.rain-tree.com/schoolreports.htm
Articles on how rainforests work, why they are so important

**www.rainforestconcern.org/education_resources/resources_
for_schools**
A guided tour of the rainforest, animated film on conservation
projects, animal photos, and much more

**video.nationalgeographic.com/video/news/140703-news-
guayusa-tea-vin?source=searchvideo**
Video on farming a sacred tea to help save the rainforest

**kids.nationalgeographic.com/explore/nature/rare-amazon-
jungle-dog**
Feature on the wild short-eared dog of the Amazon

**nature.org/ourinitiatives/regions/southamerica/brazil/
placesweprotect/amazon.xml**
Reports on efforts to save endangered plants and animals

pbs.org/journeyintoamazonia
3-hour TV series exploring the world's largest river system

- *Library research—in either the school library or public libraries*
- *Magazine and newspaper articles*
- *Trade books*
- *Historical documents*
- *Artifacts*
- *Maps*
- *Photographs, illustrations, charts*
- *Research-based fiction and creative nonfiction*

The teacher notes that some of the potential interviewees might feel more comfortable speaking in Spanish, and uses this point to emphasize the benefits of bilingualism.

Over the next several weeks, Ms. Valiente allows both classroom and homework time for completion of the project. During classroom time she rotates between groups, providing assistance and facilitation as needed. She also notes the names of knowledgeable adults that emerge from this activity, and contacts several to see if they would be willing to make presentations to the class. She is looking for guest speakers who can provide factual information, but also demonstrate skills such as traditional basket weaving, the use of musical instruments, and so on. Especially welcome would be those who can share stories, both personal anecdotes and folklore, regarding the Amazon region.

◆◆◆◆◆◆◆◆

BECAUSE THIS IS A SHELTERED SUBJECT MATTER CLASS and the students have limited English proficiency, Ms. Valiente has not emphasized text analysis or memorizing vocabulary lists, but rather ways of doing research that are authentic, relevant, and enjoyable. While fostering content knowledge, she knows that other types of growth will happen along the way, including learning to work cooperatively with others, developing research skills, and, of course, increasing English language proficiency. Through their projects to discover the Amazon, students will naturally acquire academic vocabulary, such as *deforestation, climatology, indigenous, biodiversity, conservation, parasite, epidemic, infectious, habitat, botanist, canopy, symbiosis, flora,* and *fauna.*

◆◆◆◆◆◆◆◆

After the students have finished their research, time is provided to prepare oral presentations on their findings for classmates and invited guests. A day is set aside for students to share what they have discovered, how they discovered it, what surprised them, and what they still don't know. Ms. Valiente emphasizes that the real test of success will be evident in the enthusiasm that comes from sharing their research, and from the quality of the questions it provokes.

Resources for Exploring the Amazon

Chapter Book

Go and Come Back, by Joan Abelove (a work of fiction based on a real-life indigenous community with a story line that is authentic, believable, and relevant to a unit on the Amazon)

Comic Book

www.rainforestconcern.org/files/Amazonas-Comics-English-Edition-1.pdf

Poetry and Photography

Sounds of Rain: Poems of the Amazon, by David L. Harrison

Informational Memoir

Tales of the Amazon: How the Munduruku Indians Live, by Daniel Munduruku

Folktales

Folktales of the Amazon, by Juan Carlos Galeano (a teacher resource with some mature themes)

The Wings of the Butterfly: A Tale of the Amazon Rainforest (told by Aaron Shepard, available at: www.aaronshep.com/stories/030.html)

Interactive Adventure Novel with Multiple Endings

The Worst-Case Scenario Ultimate Adventure: Amazon, by David Borgenicht and Hena Khan, with Ed Stafford, Amazon consultant

Articles with a Focus on Social Action

amazonaid.org/learn/amazon-the-beautiful

Performance Piece for Children

www.assemblies.org.uk/pri/1870/if-the-forest-could-speak

Creative Arts Ideas

Engage the Creative Arts: A Framework for Sheltering and Scaffolding Instruction for English Language Learners, by Sharon Adelman Reyes

Each presentation will be followed by a Q & A with the audience. Ms. Valiente remarks that she hopes questions will emerge that no one in the room can yet answer, stressing that unanswered questions should not embarrass the groups, but demonstrate that they have been successful in raising provocative ideas.

Most of the day is devoted to presentations by the students and their guests. Parents and relatives are in attendance. The students have decorated the room with illustrations and artifacts collected in the process of their research. The classroom furniture has been reconfigured so that everyone is seated in a semicircle, ready to focus attention on the presentations. Audiovisual equipment is available.

Each presentation—including those of the guests—is followed by an excited exchange of questions, commentary, and ideas. Everyone feels a little sad when the day concludes and the students go home. Before leaving, they decide to have a follow-up discussion the next week, to explore possibilities for further research or activism.

♦♦♦♦♦♦♦♦♦

Ms. Valiente considered a number of new directions in which the project could lead. Over the weekend, she sorted through additional resources about the Amazon Rainforest. The result was a resource list *(see sidebar, previous page)* that would help to satisfy the appetites of her students by providing multiple pathways to further explore the Amazon. Her ideas included:

- Reading chapter books, comic books, poetry, memoir, folktales, and interactive adventure novels;
- Taking part in social action, such as working to preserve the rainforest and the ways of life of indigenous peoples;
- Engaging in performance art, creative writing, and visual art projects;
- Investigating rainforests in other regions of the world;
- Researching traditional folk-arts and folklore of the Amazon;
- Exploring the topic of sustainability;

• Tracing the interconnections between climates and geographic regions around the world; and

• Considering the ethical issues of first contact with indigenous peoples and dilemmas concerning the preservation of cultures versus the advantages of a modern lifestyle.

••••••••••

All in all, Ms. Valiente is pleased, not only by all that her students have learned and experienced, but also by what she herself has learned and experienced. She knows she will continue her own learning along with theirs.

References

August, D. & Hakuta, K. (Eds.) (1997). *Improving Schooling for Language-Minority Children: A Research Agenda.* Washington, DC: National Academy Press.

Center for Applied Linguistics (n.d.a). SIOP: http://www.cal.org/siop/index.html.

Center for Applied Linguistics (n.d.b). What Is the SIOP Model? http://www.cal.org/siop/about/index.html.

Center for Applied Linguistics (n.d.c). SIOP Lesson Plans and Activities: http://www.cal.org/siop/lesson-plans/index.html.

Center for Applied Linguistics (n.d.d). Elementary Level Assessment Activity—Science: Floating and Sinking: http://www.cal.org/siop/pdfs/siop-elementary-science-activity-floating-and-sinking.pdf.

Center for Applied Linguistics (n.d.e). Taínos: SIOP Lesson Plan: http://www.cal.org/siop/pdfs/tainos.pdf.

Crawford, J. (2004). *Educating English Learners: Language Diversity in the Classroom.* Los Angeles: Bilingual Educational Services.

Cummins, J. (2001 [1979]). Research findings from French immersion programs across Canada: A parent's guide. In Baker, C. & Hornberger, N. (Eds.), *An Introductory Reader to the Writings of Jim Cummins,* (pp. 96–105). Clevedon, UK: Multilingual Matters.

Dupuy, B. (2000). Content-based instruction: Can it help ease the transition from beginning to advanced foreign language classes? *Foreign Language Annals* 33(2): 205–223.

Echevarría, J., & Graves, A. (2003). *Sheltered Content Instruction: Teaching English-Language Learners with Diverse Abilities,* 2nd Ed. Boston: Allyn & Bacon.

Echevarría, J., Short, D. & Powers, K. (2006). School reform and standards-based education: A model for English-language learners. *Journal of Educational Research* 99(4): 195–210.

Echevarría, J., Richards-Tutor, C., Chinn, V.P. & Ratleff, P.A. (2011a). Did they get it? The role of fidelity in teaching English learners. *Journal of Adolescent & Adult Literacy* 54(6): 425–434.

Echevarría, J., Richards-Tutor, C., Canges, R. & Francis, D. (2011b). Using the SIOP Model to Promote the Acquisition of Language and Science Concepts with English Learners. *Bilingual Research Journal* 34(3): 334–351.

Echevarría, J., Vogt, M. & Short, D.J. (2013). *Making Content Comprehensible for English Learners: The SIOP® Model*, 4th Ed. Boston: Pearson.

Edwards, H., Wesche, M., Krashen, S., Clement, R., and Kruidenier, B. (1984). Second language acquisition through subject-matter learning: A study of sheltered psychology classes at the University of Ottawa. *Canadian Modern Language Review* 41: 268–282.

Ellis, A.K. (2005). *Research on Educational Innovations*, 4th Ed. New York: Routledge

Falk, L. (2009). *Teaching the Way That Children Learn*. New York: Teachers College Press.

Fosnot, C.T. (2005). *Constructivism: Theory, Perspectives, and Practice,* 2nd Ed. New York: Teachers College Press.

Goldenberg, C. (2013). Unlocking the research on English learners: What we know—and don't yet know—about effective instruction. *American Educator* 37(2): 4–11, 38.

Guarino, A.J., Echevarría, J., Short, D., Schick, J.E., Forbes, S. & Rueda, R. (2001). The Sheltered Instruction Observation Protocol. *Journal of Research in Education* 11(1): 138–140.

Helping English Learners Succeed (2002). Washington, DC: Center for Applied Linguistics.

Hill, P. & Barber, M. (2014). *Preparing for a Renaissance in Assessment*. London: Pearson.

Howard, E.R., Sugarman, J. & Coburn, C. (2006). *Adapting the Sheltered Instruction Observation Protocol (SIOP) for Two-Way Immersion Education: An Introduction to the TWIOP*. Washington, DC: Center for Applied Linguistics: http://www.cal.org/twi/TWIOP.pdf.

Institute of Education Sciences, U.S. Department of Education. (2013). WWC Intervention Report: Sheltered Instruction Observation

Protocol (SIOP®): http://ies.ed.gov/ncee/wwc/
interventionreport.aspx?sid=460.

Johnson, S.B., Blum, R.W. & Giedd, J.N. (2009). Adolescent maturity
and the brain: The promise and pitfalls of neuroscience research
in adolescent health policy. *Journal of Adolescent Health,* 45(3):
216–221.

Krashen, S. (1984). Immersion: Why it works and what it has taught
us. *Language & Society* 12 (Winter): 61–64.

Krashen, S. (1985). *The Input Hypothesis.* London & New York:
Longman.

Krashen, S. (1991). Sheltered subject matter teaching. *Cross Currents*
18 (Winter): 185–189. Rpt. in Oller, J.W. (Ed.), *Methods That Work:
Ideas for Literacy and Language Teachers* (pp. 143–148). Boston:
Heinle & Heinle, 1993.

Krashen, S. (2001). Bilingual education: Arguments for and (bogus)
arguments against. In Alatis, J. & Tan, A-H. (Eds.), *Language in
Our Time: Bilingual Education and Official English, Ebonics and
Standard English, Immigration and the Unz Initiative.*
Washington, DC: Georgetown University Press.

Krashen, S. (2003). *Explorations in Language Acquisition and Use: The
Taipei Lectures.* Portsmouth, NH: Heinemann.

Krashen, S. (2004). *The Power of Reading: Insights from the Research,*
2nd Ed. Portsmouth, NH & Westport, CT: Heinemann & Libraries
Unlimited.

Krashen, S. (2011). The compelling (not just interesting) input
hypothesis. *The English Connection* 15(3): 1.

Krashen, S. (2013). Does research support SIOP's claims?
International Journal of Foreign Language Teaching 8(1): 11.

Krashen, S. (2014). Case histories and the Comprehension Hypothesis.
TESOL International Journal 9(1): March.

Madeline Cheek Hunter (1916–1994). Education Encyclopedia,
StateUniversity.com: http://education.stateuniversity.com/
pages/2074/Hunter-Madeline-Cheek-1916-1994.html.

McField, G. & McField, D. (2014). The consistent outcome of bilingual
education programs: A meta-analysis of meta-analyses. In

McField, G. (Ed.), *The Miseducation of English Learners.* Charlotte, NC: Information Age Publishing, pp. 267–299.

McIntyre, E., Kyle, D., Chen, C-T., Muñoz, M. & Beldon, S. (2010). Teacher learning and ELL reading achievement in sheltered instruction classrooms: Linking professional development to student development. *Literacy Research & Instruction* 49: 334–351.

McLaughlin, B. (1987). *Theories of Second Language Learning.* London: Edward Arnold.

Meier, D. (1995). *The Power of Their Ideas: Lessons for America from a Small School in Harlem.* Boston: Beacon Press.

O'Shea, T. (2013). Minerals: http://www.thedoctorwithin.com/minerals/minerals.

Pearson (2010). "Who Took My Chalk?" March 31: http://www.eschoolnews.com/2010/03/31/who-took-my-chalk-pearson-the-edventure-group-launch-new-teacher-professional-development-program.

Pearson (2012). Annual Report and Accounts: http://ar2012.pearson.com/assets/downloads/15939_PearsonAR12.pdf.

Pearson (2013). What has the latest research on the SIOP Model shown? [video]: https://www.youtube.com/watch?v=JbbGlklFLw0&sns=tw.

Pearson (n.d.a). ELL and SIOP®: http://www.pearsonschool.com/index.cfm?locator=PS1sAt.

Pearson (n.d.b). About the SIOP® Model: http://siop.pearson.com/about-siop/index.html.

Pearson (n.d.c) SIOP Institute FAQ: http://www.pearsonschool.com/index.cfm?locator=PS1sCe.

Quinton, L. & McGee, K. (2013) What's in Texas' $500 Million Contract with Pearson? July 16. http://kut.org/post/what-s-texas-500-million-testing-contract-pearson.

Reyes, S.A. (2013). *Engage the Creative Arts: A Framework for Sheltering and Scaffolding Instruction for English Language Learners.* Portland, OR: DiversityLearningK12.

Reyes, S.A. & Crawford, J. (2012). *Diary of a Bilingual School: How a Constructivist Curriculum, a Multicultural Perspective, and a*

Commitment to Dual Immersion Education Combined to Foster Fluent Bilingualism in Spanish- and English-Speaking Children. Portland, OR: DiversityLearningK12.

Rolstad, K., Mahoney, K. & Glass G. (2005). The big picture: A meta-analysis of program effectiveness research on English language learners. *Educational Policy* 19(4): 572–594

Saunders, W. & Goldenberg, C. (2010). Research to guide English language development instruction. In *Improving Education for English Learners: Research Based Approaches* (pp. 21–81). Sacramento: California Department of Education.

Short, D.J., Fidelman, C.G. & Louguit, M. (2012). Developing academic language in English language learners through sheltered instruction. *TESOL Quarterly* 46(2): 334–361.

Swain, M. & Lapkin, S. (1995). Problems in output and the cognitive processes they generate: A step towards second language learning. *Applied Linguistics* 16: 371–391.

Zehr, M.A. (2006). 'No Child' impact on English-learners mulled. *Education Week,* March 1, pp. 1, 14–15.

About the Authors

JAMES CRAWFORD, former Washington editor of *Education Week,* is an independent writer and advocate on issues affecting English language learners. He is the founding president of the Institute for Language and Education Policy. Previously he served as executive director of the National Association for Bilingual Education. He is the author of numerous publications, including *Educating English Learners (5th Ed.), Language Loyalties, Hold Your Tongue,* and *At War with Diversity.* Currently he is president of DIVERSITYLEARNINGK12, a consulting group that provides professional development, keynote presentations, program design, educational publishing, and related services.

Crawford has given keynote speeches and other invited presentations at professional conferences, universities, and school districts in more than 30 states and several foreign countries. He is webmaster and web designer of www.languagepolicy.net, www.diversitylearningk12.com, and www.elladvocates.org.

He graduated with an A.B., cum laude, from Harvard College in 1971. In 2009, he was awarded an honorary Doctorate of Humane Letters by DePaul University.

SHARON ADELMAN REYES, treasurer of the Institute for Language and Education Policy, holds a PH.D. in curriculum design from the University of Illinois at Chicago, where she specialized in multicultural and bilingual education. Over a career spanning more than 35 years, she has worked as a teacher, principal, curriculum specialist, program evaluator, district administrator, college professor, and educational researcher. She has taught at the preschool, elementary, secondary, and university levels and was awarded the Kohl International Prize for Exemplary Teaching for her work as a K–8 teacher of English as a second language in the Chicago Public Schools.

Besides serving as both an ESL and a self-contained classroom teacher for 12 years, Reyes has worked as a fine arts specialist and an English teacher. She has taught in multiple contexts, including work with children, youth, and parents in Latino and African-American communities and in multicultural settings. Since 1999, Reyes has provided direct assistance to K–12 schools serving low-income communities to improve curriculum and instruction in ESL, dual immersion, transitional bilingual education, and literacy programs. While consulting in school districts throughout the United States, she has developed, guided, and evaluated programs, provided teachers with field support and professional development workshops, and worked closely with school administrators to facilitate these efforts.

Reyes is author of *Engage the Creative Arts: A Framework for Sheltering and Scaffolding Instruction for English Language Learners* and coauthor of *Diary of a Bilingual School; Teaching in Two Languages: A Guide for K–12 Bilingual Educators;* and *Constructivist Strategies for Teaching English Language Learners.* She served as lead editor of *La Palabra Justa: An English-Spanish / Español-Inglés Glossary of Academic Vocabulary for Bilingual Teaching & Learning.* Her publications also include peer-reviewed journal articles, magazine pieces, and curriculum guides.

While holding academic positions at St. Xavier and Loyola Chicago universities, Reyes developed undergraduate and graduate programs in bilingual-bicultural education and ESL, and a graduate program in educational leadership in English-learner contexts. She has presented in her field locally, nationally, and internationally. Her current research interests include the preparation of teachers and administrators for diverse classrooms, constructivist practice in ELL contexts, bilingual schooling, and educational leadership. She is now program director of DIVERSITY-LEARNINGK12.

About ILEP

The Institute for Language and Education Policy,
founded in 2006, is a nonprofit organization dedicated
to promoting educational equity and excellence for
English language learners. We are teachers,
administrators, researchers, professors, students, and
others who believe that the time for advocacy is now.
In an era of misguided "accountability" measures,
high-stakes testing, cutbacks in school funding, and
English Only activism, strong advocacy for children is
essential. Scientific knowledge about what works –
not ideology or political expedience – must guide
public policy. For more information, please visit us at
www.elladvocates.org
or email us at
info@elladvocates.org.

28287144R00061

Made in the USA
Middletown, DE
08 January 2016